OPEN WOUNDS

CHRISTOPHER ALLEN

Ascension Publishing, LLC

OPEN WOUNDS

© 2015 by Christopher L. Allen. All rights reserved.

Published by Ascension Publishing, LLC
ascensionpublishingllc@gmail.com

Ordering Information:

Quantity sales. Special discounts are available on quantity purchases by corporations, associations, and others. Orders made by U.S. trade bookstores and wholesalers, please contact the publisher referencing Sales at ascensionpublishingllc@gmail.com or by Tel: 804-464-8479.

Cover Illustration/Photo Adobe Stock

Cover Design by Irosh

Editing by: Dr. Meldon Jenkins-Jones

All rights reserved. No part of this book may be reproduced, utilized, or transmitted in any form or by any means, including internet usage without written permission of the Ascension Publishing, LLC, or the author. Permission requests should be addressed to the publisher, Permissions Department, Ascension Publishing, LLC at ascensionpublishingllc@gmail.com

Library of Congress Catalog Number: 2017913131

ISBN: 978-0-692-30866-0

1. Poetry   2. Self Help

PRINTED IN THE UNITED STATES OF AMERICA

Dedication

      I dedicate this book to my parents, Linda A. Richardson, and the late James A. Richardson for being great examples to me even when I didn't fully understand or know what lessons were being taught to me in my times of hurt, rebellion and imperfection.

      Linda, thank you for your unceasing support, love, and guidance. Thank you for being consistent and never changing as a person. You have always responded with respect, kindness, and truth.

      James *Dean*, thank you for your patience and teaching me what it is to be a good, honest, and hardworking man. I misplaced those values and teachings briefly. They have been rediscovered and applied to every aspect of my life.

      This book is also dedicated to the adult and young men who mean well but are stuck in their pasts and have difficulty moving forward positively in their lives. For the young ladies and women that love and support these men this is also dedicated to you. This book will help you have a better understanding of what these males may be going through. I am in hope that this information will ultimately reduce additional baggage and traumas to your relationships with them and reduce further judgment upon them on their journeys toward growth and being better men.

Acknowledgement

First and foremost, I thank God and all my teachers, both human and divine for guiding me through all the trenches, peaks, and valleys of my life. Without you I wouldn't be who I am today nor be in a position to share my experiences to inspire personal growth, hope and positive changes in the lives of those that read this book.

To my wife, Sonya Allen, female version of my best friend, confidant, partner, and soul mate. Thank you for your huge heart, outlook on life, undying support, vision, and encouragement.

To my beautiful daughters, Kristen, and Minuette: thank you for your patience, unconditional love, and support. Without you both, I would not have had the courage to step out of my comfort zone to become a better man, parent and to make better life choices. I love and thank you both!

To my brothers, sisters, aunts, uncles, cousins, nieces, nephews, in-laws, and friends you have all played very important roles in my life and development. Thank you for your prayers and support over the years! God bless you all!

To my brothers from another mother: Eric Laws, Cornel Enoch, Eric Cooper, Michael Collier, Dion Henriques, Theotis Joe, Jr., Tim Jones, Sr., William Walker, Big Merce, Stephon Teel, Anthony Hoyte, Russel Blanding, the Bag Boyz, and the Men's Huddle, thank you for being there for me through thick and thin. I couldn't have asked for a better group of men to support and grow with me over the years.

I want to acknowledge and thank all of those who have supported, inspired, and given me great advice and the drive to finish what I have started. Continue your blessed and anointed paths, showering the world with your creative gifts: Raymond "Alex" Miller, David Ware, Janel "Sapphire" Ricks, Lesley "Lez" Tyson, Holly Johnson, Terri Hope, Shandah Owens, Lady Eros, Sandra Wilson, Valerie McAllister, Tameeka Lesley, Kula Voncille, Rodney Allen, Omilade Davis, Sylvia Carr, Shervon Smith-Sonnebeyatta, Glynis Boyd-Hughes, Gary Hughes, Gwen "Starr" Holloway, Gee Gee Baldwin, Stacey Thomas, Hakeem Gilliam El, Miasha Gilliam El, Kevin Jackson, Black Fonzarelli, Cornelius "Soloman Grundy" Brown, Carla Echevarria Savage, Robert Hall, Mark Dowrite, Darlene A. Scott, Chris Claiborne, Minoka Smith, Tiffany Austin, Hoke S. Glover III, Vincent Bungy, LaSonya Wiggins, Kevin Keel, Tarron Richardson, Loretta Richardson, James "Shane" Richardson, Theresa Richardson, Aunt Polly, Bessie "Aunt Lil" Collick, Terry Evans, Edward Hall, Carmen Hall, Tervon Fletcher-Caldwell, Sharon Oliver, the E.B.O. Family, the Book Club Cast, and Crew.

To all of my family and friends who are with me in spirit, you're greatly loved, cherished, and missed! Continue to blow wind my way!

For those that have supported and been with me over the years and I failed to mention, please forgive me.

Introduction to the Readers

The "OPEN WOUNDS" series are great support tools and read for young males and adult men who mean well but are stuck in their pasts and have difficulty moving forward positively in life. It is also an introduction to address and bring closure to those who are still trying to make sense of it all. Those who are still asking why me? Those still living and surviving with *open wounds*. Many of the wounds we have experienced were beyond our control, and some were simply self-inflicted.

In my experience, hurt people hurt other people. As human beings, we purposely and inadvertently project our thoughts, emotions, and experiences onto others, not understanding that your thoughts, behaviors, and actions will come back to you in some form or another.

If I continued to play the victim, stay angry, blame others, and live-in depression and hopelessness, I would remain stuck in my own mental prison, recycling unhealthy attitudes, bad behaviors, and broken relationships. If you are lost or hurt, take the time to find yourself. Be still, heal and reflect before lashing out at others or doing something that you will regret.

I cannot change what has happened in the past, but I have control over myself, my outlook on life and how I feel. I learned that my value in life, self-esteem, and character are not based on my past or what people perceive me to be. Who are you today? Each morning is a brand-new day to rebuild and rebrand your life. Open up and begin to love yourself and others. Forgive yourself and those who have caused you harm or pain. Let go of the past and it will let go of you. Once you know better do better. Make the world around you a better place to live and in turn, you will experience the same. You only have one chance at living this life. Why not make it a great one!

OPEN WOUNDS
Table of Contents

Dedication iv

Acknowledgement..v

Introduction to the Readers vii

Table of Contents viii

C H A P T E R 1 12

Written Off Prematurely 13

God, Where Are You?...14

I Am Proud to Say...15

An Act of Kindness 16

It Wasn't My Imagination 18

Snakes in the Pulpit..19

Grandmother 22

If Only I Had Listened 23

The First Time We Met...25

The Answers I Sought...26

The Effects of His Absence 28

School Daze 31

Like Clairvoyance..33

She's Not Pregnant*...35

Thanks, Coach 42

Kim 47

Tested*..49

C H A P T E R 2 53

My Vice..54

My Special Friend 55
My Woman's Gone 56
Grown and Opinionated 58
Caught Up.. 59
I Used to Be Him... 61
Divine Intervention I... 63
Divine Intervention II*.. 64
Divine Intervention III... 67
It's All Good 73
My Money 75
To Prove a Point 77
In My Past Life 78
No Love 79
Blurred Lines 79
The Forecast 80
My Diagnosis 81
The Situation 83
The Situation II 84
Guilty by Association 85
Conflicted 89
Reasons of Uncertainty 90
360 Degrees 92
Sincerely Yours (The Boomerang Affect).............................. 94
The Corridor of Contemplation 95
In the Dark.. 96
Consumed with Worry 102
Informed Decision 103

Selfish	104
Did She Consider	105
The Perfectly Placed Call*	106
Mistaken Identity	109
Isolated	111
Violated	113
Euthanized	115
This Is Not Love	116
The Wrong Person	117
Romance	118
I'm So Tired	119
I Didn't Leave Because of You	119
Black and White	120
When a Woman Cares	121
Looking Out	122
Looking Out II	126
Fun Dummy	128
The Breaking Point	129
Hopeless and Broken	130
C H A P T E R 3	132
Awakening	133
Compartmentalized	134
I Made a Mistake	136
I'm Sorry	137
Who Do You Have to Blame?	138
The Loss of Choice and Freedom	139
Badge of Honor	140

My Girl's Friends Confession 142

Just for the Moment 143

Acceptance and Forgiveness 144

The Urban Male Disorder 145

Put Down the Gun 146

In My Opinion 147

Desensitized 148

Separated 149

Change 151

The Truth 151

Often, I Find Myself 152

Sometimes 153

Complacent Breeze 154

Idle Time 155

Your Legacy 156

In Reflection 157

About the Author 159

Contact Information 160

Stoetry *is a combination of poetry and short stories in one work. The titles are marked with an asterisk**

CHAPTER 1

Written Off Prematurely

Medical books and doctors say I was born prematurely
But I say I was born in perfect timing
January 29, 1971
2lbs 4 ounces
Nearly five inches in length
My mother went through excruciating pain during my birth
Because I was physically too weak
To help her bring me into this world
At birth, I was written off prematurely
I was assumed to be stillborn
Because I didn't move, cry, or make any noise at first
My heartbeat was nearly too faint to be detected
My mother was told I wouldn't make it
My chances of survival were slim to none
I wasn't expected to survive the night
The doctors said I was born too small and too soon
I had no weight, and I was too weak to survive
The doctors said my internal organs might not be developed
Enough to keep me alive on my own
At birth, I was written off prematurely
I fought, I survived, I am here
My family members held me in the palms of their hands
I was too small to be cradled in their arms or chest
My mother and the hospital staff had to make handmade diapers
Out of cloth or whatever was available
Because there were no diapers made in my size
Each diaper was held closed with a small safety pin
At birth, I was written off prematurely
I fought
I survived
I am here
Look at me now

Your life's story doesn't have to equate to or end the way that it started! Through our sickness and health, understand and learn what it is to live, but live to be alive, not just survive! Always remember that!

God, Where Are You?

Why do infants and good people have to suffer and die?
Why is there so much hurt and pain in the world?
Why is there so much sickness and disease?
Why are people allowed to be taken into slavery
In this modern-day era?
Why are there millions of people going hungry
And starving all over the world?
Why are our nations threatening
And going to war over trivial things?
Why are the nations of the world so divided?
The world says they believe in you
But why do people commit heinous crimes in your name?
Why does skin color and money determine your worth?
Why does man destroy nature and
Everything he gets his hands on for control and profit?
Are you listening?
I pray to you almost every night
Why don't you answer or respond?
God, where are you?
I can't see you.
If you're real you could stop all this pain, destruction
And nonsense in an instant
God, where are you?

I was shielded from the realities of life until I wasn't. There will be times when you feel hurt and abandoned. There will be times when you question everything. There will be times when you doubt yourself, lose faith in religion and the higher powers that be. When you feel this way, you are not alone. Your inner guide will always prompt you to ask the difficult questions and seek truth as you are awakened to the true nature of this existence.

I Am Proud to Say

Sad as it may seem
I saw and experienced with my grandmother's generation
Her children's generation and their children's generation
Pray for equality and better treatment
Then march on
Clench fists and lay hands on
Grab rocks, bricks, knives, forks, bottles, pots, tree limbs, snub
noses, and shotguns to defend the skin they were in
Just to enjoy the necessities and liberties in life
Like sitting on our porches
Buying groceries from the store
Using public restrooms
Driving into or passing predominantly
Caucasian neighborhoods
Waiting to ride the local buses
Walking to and from school
Or just going outside to play in any neighborhood or public park
There was a high chance of being harassed, shot at, kicked,
Punched, Jumped, stabbed and
Called derogatory names, threatened, spit at, spit on or killed
Just for being born naturally with melanated skin
I am proud to have seen and been a part of that struggle
Where my family stood up for themselves and did what was right,
FIGHT!

I was raised to be kind, loving and respectful to others no matter their color, gender, religion or beliefs. I was taught never to provoke or start a conflict, but by all means end it with respect to the law.

An Act of Kindness

As early as I could remember I was taught to ignore the ignorant. The ignorant comments coming from racist white folk like tar baby, spook, coon, and nigger. Go back to Africa, go back to where you came from, you don't belong here and get out of my neighborhood. As if white people purchased and owned all the houses and land in our communities. It was becoming unbearable to hold it all in and not fight. It was hard not to say anything hateful back to them. Sometimes tears would stream down my face out of pure frustration, but I found more room inside to swallow just a little bit more.

There were times when the younger Caucasian children wanted to talk and play with me. They didn't see color as an issue. If they were caught, they were punished or beaten, driving this senseless hate home. At the same time the racists' children began to hate and resent their parents and grandparents for hurting them for being children.

One of the most notorious, loudmouth, racist fathers that lived in my grandmother's neighborhood, Simon's Garden, walked into the community store with his son and daughter. The two were savagely beaten for playing with me a few days before. Their marks were still fresh as if it happened that morning. At nine years old I couldn't wait to grow up so that I could kick his ass if he were still alive. I was waiting on three Hamburger Combos that I ordered for my brother, dad, and myself for lunch. My brother and I were working for our father repairing his mother's roof to earn spending money and learn a trade. The racist father damn near walked through me as he passed by asking to speak to the owner of the store. He wanted to extend his open tab for some bread, milk, and a few other items. The owner's wife told him that her husband wasn't there, and his tab was closed until he paid off what was previously owed. He scowled and argued with her, demanding an extension. She told him to leave, or she was going to call the police.

I knew she had a shotgun close by in the store. She could have brandished and cocked it to make him leave the store, but she was thinking maternally not to traumatize the two kids any further. The son and daughter started to cry in the confusion saying they were hungry and scared. I felt angry, sad, and compelled to help at the same time. As ugly as he was, I couldn't let his children and my friends go hungry for his acts of entitlement, arrogance, and ignorance. Risking getting in trouble for spending money that wasn't mine, I asked the owner's wife, "How much it would cost for their groceries?"

She said, "Eight dollars and ninety-seven cents!"

He must have had a huge bill or a history of not paying his dues. I gave her a ten-dollar bill of my father's money and waited for the change. His children looked at him, waiting for him to say thank you, but he never did. For a few seconds, I could see in his eyes that he wanted to say something kind, but because of embarrassment, how he treated others, and his pride, he just looked at me in bewilderment. He grabbed the grocery bag and proceeded to leave the store. The owner's wife snarled at him and said, "You're not even going to say thank you? Young man you did a very nice thing for someone who didn't deserve it." Afterwards, she put my order in a bag and gave me a separate bag for the three drinks. I felt good inside, but I had to deal with another situation. I had to muster up enough courage to tell my father I used eight dollars and ninety-seven cents of his money, without asking, to help someone who didn't deserve it and despised us.

Despite his or her shortcomings, treat people the way you want to be treated. You will have favor because of it. Regardless of our beliefs, the individuals you despise, may be of aid or may save your life one day!

It Wasn't My Imagination

At a young age I was privileged to another world or reality
Many wished not to talk about
The things I could sense
The beings I saw
The places they took me
The things I was told and
The things I knew
We are not alone, but I was told I was hearing and seeing things
It wasn't my imagination
Being with them
Being out there, wherever that was
I felt like I was at home
It was peaceful, safe, and secure
I was happy and free
I never felt more alive, but when I came back here
I was alone, miserable, and utterly lost
I have always felt like I didn't belong here and
It was hard trying to explain the unexplainable to someone
Who didn't understand or believe that
There is so much going on beyond what our eyes can see
It wasn't my imagination
I hated to have dreams or visions of those I was close to
The majority of dreams and visions were good, but many were bad
I knew these gifts were meant to be helpful
But it wasn't perceived as such
Revealing this information took courage
Knowing that you would be teased or
Possibly cursed out or worse
I was called a freak, a demon, and a male witch
Many people thought I was putting on for attention
I was told to stop watching scary movies and Sci-Fi TV
I was considered too young to know anything or be respected
It was supposedly all in my head
I was told to be quiet
I was told to go about my business
Until what I said kept happening
Who's crazy now?
But I was told, it was all my imagination

Snakes in the Pulpit

Less than 12 years of age
My expectations of the persons orchestrating the church
Should have been equal to the standard I was held to
Inside and outside of church
I was told to be on my best behavior at all times
Because I'd never know who I was entertaining and
I'd never know who was watching

Do as I say, not as I do must have been the church's slogan, but
I wasn't fooled by the snakes growing
In the high grass amongst the pews and pulpit
Feasting and thriving on hate, greed, competition
Confusion, insecurities, lust, and jealousies
Their sweet and charming voices spoke verses
With spontaneity or after rehearses
But their behaviors were in reverse like cars backing up

The things I saw and
Experienced in church made me not want to go back
When I got of age, I didn't go back
I envisioned the church to be a place of sanctuary and peace
A place for repentance
A place for forgiveness
A place of unconditional love and acceptance
A place to gather my strength and
Put on my spiritual armor for the upcoming weeks
But weekly, I was drained like boiled potatoes and noodles for salad
There was no real forgiveness, repentance, or unconditional love
Members there couldn't wait to get out of the church doors
Like demons made to sit on the pews laced with holy water
Ready to curse, drink, smoke, fight or start some shit
Soldiers for God,
More like hypocrites using God's name for self
They soiled the teachings of the Bible
Like Port-A-Potties at a Michael Jackson concert outdoors overseas

Because my interpretation of the Bible was
Contrary to what the elders taught and believed
I was told not to ask any questions in Sunday school and service
So, I used my best judgment
I didn't believe that Mary had gotten pregnant on her own
To me, someone sneaked Mary while she was sleeping or
Passed out after drinking wine or
She may have been artificially inseminated by someone
Or something
I am a believer in miracles, but
Women don't impregnate themselves
And if God made us in their image, male and female
Why does the Bible reflect that she wasn't there in the beginning?
I felt that he had a mate too and female entities in heaven a well.
It just didn't make sense to me that
If God created all the other species and gave them a mate
That he didn't have a mate of his own in Heaven

I know the church can't run on its own, but
It really made me upset that the elderly was on Social Security
Paying full tithes
Some men and women in the church
Didn't have a steady place to live
And were in danger of losing their residences
Or their utilities were in danger of being cut off
Many members had minimum wage jobs
And just managed to scrape up what they could
To put into the offering plate
Families struggled to make it with no assistance from the Church
The congregation was baited into giving their last or was made to
Feel bad for not giving 500, 250, 100, 75, 50 or
25 dollars per person
If you were not children
Anything less than 20 dollars, keep it in your pocket or be criticized
Where you stand
It was a rare thing to see acts of kindness given to the congregation

That gave everything they had to a snake and pimp in the pulpit
Members and associates of the congregation
Stabbed each other in the back with gossip knives
They looked like porcupines or someone receiving acupuncture
Then turn around and say trust in me
I love you brother
I love you sister
I got your back
We are friends
If this is what they call
Fellowship, love, togetherness, and friendship
I don't want any part of it
But one thing that I learned from this experience is that
The world will be the world and people are going to be people
I'm not responsible for their behaviors or salvation
I am responsible for my own

There are so many lessons to digest and learn from this poem. Watch the company you keep - Friends, foes and frienemies - Words vs. Actions - Real vs. Fake – Respect vs. Disrespect - Don't judge others - Be responsible for your own actions - Control and manipulation is not love - Taking advantage of the vulnerable – Abuse of title and status – Do as I say, not as I do (You will not gain the listeners respect this way)

Grandmother

    I told her almost everything because she asked me. I didn't see or feel any harm in it. I talked to her because she would listen. I talked to her openly because I was her grandson. I believed she genuinely cared. I told her things about me in total confidence. I didn't know she was a person I couldn't talk to. My heart and trust in her were broken the day she sent me to Eckerd Drug's Store to get a jar of Folger's Coffee and two hard packs of Benson and Hedges Cigarettes with matches. I rushed back to the apartment to catch the beginning of my favorite Saturday morning cartoon. Upon entering the apartment, I heard her on the phone telling someone and laughing hysterically about a sensitive and personal matter I discussed with her. It was regarding my first stages of puberty. I was hurt, disappointed and angry with her. She made me feel like I was the brunt of a joke towards an enemy or someone she didn't care about. That day I learned there was no true anonymity or confidentiality in her. She spewed everything she heard like the effects of food poisoning on the stomach. I wondered how many times she had done this to her family, and friends. I told myself I will be alright, but deep down inside I wasn't. My heart and trust in her went missing like the children shown on posters and milk cartons for years to come.

Be careful of who you talk to and trust, even with someone else's personal business! It's all fun and games until the situation is flipped on you!

If Only I Had Listened

I lost count of how many times my mother told me to stop jumping down the stairs and sliding down the banisters. One day someone is going to get hurt. We lived in 3-C, which was on the third floor of our apartment building. If you slipped between the banisters, there was quite a fall to the basement floor. If you bounced off a banister onto a hallway floor, you were lucky. The blah, blah, blah was in one ear and out the other. I heard what she was saying but it was fun. I was fearless and invincible.

It was early Thursday evening, and I just finished my homework. I was eager to go outside and catch the remaining daylight with my friends just before dinner. Heading outside, I ran full speed toward the banister and took flight. I'm not sure how long I was out of it, but I woke up very groggy on the basement floor of our building. Yellow, blue, green, white, and red stars danced emphatically in front of my eyes to the growing pain occupying the circumference of my entire head. I couldn't see them, but I felt several large strawberries tingling in my back, ribs, arms, and legs as I began to regain my senses. I tried to sit up vertically. A searing pain shot through my right arm, and I had never felt anything like this before. I couldn't move it without assistance from my left arm. There was no strength in it. I had to keep my arm cradled close to my body to move it, but the pain intensified by the second.

If I had only listened, I wouldn't have run into the house screaming like a banshee. I scared my mother half to death.

My mother ran out of the kitchen screaming frantically, "Chris, what happened to you?"

As I told her what happened there was no compassion at all. She smacked me like I was being disciplined for everything I was never caught doing. Maybe it was the combination of her being frustrated with trying to keep her children out of avoidable situations. Maybe she was frustrated with repeating herself, don't do this, don't do that. Maybe she was frustrated with having a chronic diabetic daughter that never ate or took her insulin properly. My sister kept her in and out of doctors' offices and hospitals at times when she should have been at work, relaxing or tending to us.

If I had only listened, I wouldn't have put my parents in a position where the school I was attending, and the doctor's office contacted Child Protective Services. They believed my parents had abused me because of the two types of breaks in my right arm. Our explanations were ignored, and it took several home visits, interviews with family, neighbors, and friends to exonerate my parents from the abuse claim. I was blessed not to be removed from my home. This would have never happened if I had only listened.

A hard head makes a soft behind! The person(s) entrusted to keep you safe can't do their job if you don't let them!

The First Time We Met

You were not considered taboo
You were discussed at school and in my household
You were off limits to me for good reasons
Like watching porn or
Hanging around troublesome neighbors down the street
But I often wondered how you tasted
I had no idea how you would affect me
I saw the changes in adult's behavior after having a few of you
During holidays, game nights and family functions
I did not see the harm in being giddy, silly, and full of laughter
But sometimes there was that family member or guest
That agitated those they were around and
Started arguments and fights
So, the gatherings and invites became less and less over the years
The older children in the family introduced me to the waiting game
It wasn't a game, but
A way to drink alcohol like adults without getting caught
If you were asked to get a beer, or mixed drink
Fix it and serve it as requested
After several drinks, the adults will ask for another one
But didn't remember if they had received it
So, we shared and sipped some
You didn't have to drink none
But your popularity amongst the younger family dropped drastically
We had plenty of candy and gum on hand
To cover up our breath if the breath tests came
We risked having a belt smacked across our frame
Having our name called and embarrassed like the wall of shame
Then be grounded for months like broken planes
We were never supposed to meet at all
But doing so, changed my life forever

The Answers I Sought

Horrifying were the facts laid before my eyes
In dreams and nightmares
Gifts undaunted by his menacing presence
Bestowed me with visions of violence that impacted my life like
Being shot by several forty caliber rounds
I wasn't there physically at first
I was informed and disturbed in the womb
I was a witness to the increasing accounts of cruelty
And domestic violence
The abuse was nonconsensual and unwarranted but
Forced on my mother by his words, hands, feet or
Whatever he could find to assault her
He claimed that he was provoked and
His behaviors were conveniently blamed on spirits
So, it was the spirits that assaulted my mother and not him
He would swear the drinking, abuse and
Hanging in the streets would stop but
I guess promises were made to be broken
Because he never kept them

Memories of previous nights were erased by blackouts
All forgotten in drunken hazes
But he had to take notice of the collateral damage the next morning
The broken furniture, glass, and damaged walls
Discoloration of bruises on the face and skin of a beautiful woman
Fearful, am I doomed to repeat the behaviors of my father?

I never hated him
I just despised his behaviors and how he treated us
When I got older, I just wanted to hear the truth from him
I wanted to find out why he did what he did to us
Like festering boils breaking the skin
It hurt like hell that my biological couldn't be truthful and
Admit to what he had done
I was a boy who was searching for answers and needing closure
To a fissure of pain, subjugated abuse, and abandonment
I never got a yes or a no
Not even a direct answer or explanation
He pretended it didn't happen
Like Flight Attendants, the US Government or Law Enforcement
Dealing with reported sightings of UFO's
Maybe it was too painful for him to admit
Even so, why am I making excuses for him?
I forgave him a long time ago
I'm just sorry the truth and the answers I sought
Didn't come from him but I must move on
I must let it all go
I must be a better man than he ever was
To my mother and I

As youth and adults, we must be careful not to become consumed in our pain and become what we despise the most. It is a must that we learn to manage our pain and frustrations and not repeat what we are experiencing or displace it on others. Forgiveness is key to our growth and development in every aspect of our lives.

The Effects of His Absence

Up until I was a teenager
I only had one Polaroid of my biological father
It seemed resistant to fading
Until the photograph casing peeled away over time
Now exposed, my fingerprints altered the colors in the picture's
Perimeter and advanced toward its center
My father's image eventually dissolved away like my patience and
Unconditional openness to accepting his absence
But in my heart
He was still prized like the 1948, Jackie Robinson Rookie Card
If there were hundreds of men gathering
Downtown in Rodney Square, Delaware
I could pick my father out in a crowd
Faster than a hummingbird flapping its wings
I'm certain he couldn't do the same if the roles were reversed
The closest I got to him was wishful thinking
Fueled by my imagination of what could have been
Like him teaching me how to ride a bike, shoot hoops, catch a
football, and hold my hands if I needed to protect myself
I was hurt in every aspect of being a young boy
And I often wondered why he never spent time with me
I made up excuses for him, but did I do it for my sanity?
Excuses that didn't make sense, but they were my excuses
Giving him more credit than he deserved
I blamed myself for my father not being in my life
Maybe it was for the better.
Day after day, his absence, and my longing for his attention
Consumed my mind like lions sharing a kill
He didn't come today because I was put on punishment and

He wasn't allowed to see me
He didn't show up this week because he was angry at me
For losing a toy figure he bought for me some time ago
He didn't come get me this time because he had to work weekends
His home phone wasn't working and
He couldn't call my mother to make arrangements to pick me up
His car broke down and he couldn't find a ride to come get me
Maybe somebody made a mistake and gave him the wrong address
After several years of this there were no more excuses
The explanations became repetitive with slight variances and
I realized he wasn't coming at all
The truth is he was angry with my mother because she
Filed for divorce and child support
She also filed a restraining order against him
Because of the domestic violence
Although he was ordered to pick me up at specific times and dates
He never adhered to any of them or wanted to pay child support
I remember waiting at rest stops and designated areas with my
Stepfather, aunt, or grandmother for several hours and
He never showed up
Like a tennis match
With anticipation, my head would turn back and forth
At each vehicle that would come into the designated area
Each time I held back tears not to cry
Each time he pulled out my loving and innocent heart
Like it was a bare ass and whooped it mercilessly
I didn't do anything to deserve this treatment and abandonment
All I wanted to do was spend time with my father
Not be caught up in his cynical and vengeful games

Every time he thought he was hurting her
He was tormenting and hurting me
I was never a priority in his life because
He put his personal issues and animosity over his son
He played a terrible game that went on far too long
If he couldn't have my mother
Although he helped to create half of me
He didn't want anything to do with me
He was afforded every opportunity to be with his son
He chose not to
Adding to an astronomical number of biological fathers
Minimizing the effects of his absence

Biological fathers, please find a way to be in your child or children's lives in a loving and constructive way, minus your personal issues and challenges! They need you to be a positive, selfless, and active influence in their lives!

School Daze

At a young age
Prior guidance, and house rules left me with decisions to make
Either stay within my parent's good graces,
Be placed on punishment
Or be greeted where your backside meets the seat
In school or on the streets, there is no reprieve
School Daze brings haze
Every day you had to defend yourself or fight
If you were getting good grades, dressed less than fashionable
Physically challenged, talked different
Came from a different state, weren't in a gang
Didn't smoke, do drugs, or sell them
You weren't considered to be shit and you were treated as such
Like the terms of an agreement
You were subject to change, derogatory changes in your name
You were targeted for kicks and fists to the body and brain
Have kids mentally, physically, and emotionally sprained
This happened before, during and after School Daze
There are so many conflicting thoughts and
Emotions brewing inside
So many decisions to make in a blink of an eye
This treatment has gone far beyond ego and pride
There will not be any teasing or conversations this time
I have been bullied or jumped one too many times
Not to disregard my parents or the *Most High*
But today I will be giving what I will be receiving
When I get home later that night
I will be taking two eyes for an eye
Giving haze to their school day
One, two or three at a time

Parents and guardians please take the time to remind our youth that school is a place of learning and collaboration. Teach our youth to be respectful, kind, and mindful of one other. Team up with the Teachers to create a unified community to ensure increasing participation and graduation rates of our children. Youth and teens, if all possible, walk away from confrontational situations! The penalty for bullying and fighting are too severe! Don't go around instigating arguments or fights, but by all means protect yourself!

Like Clairvoyance

Like clairvoyance
Prior to the phone ringing
I knew who was calling and for what
Truth be told she was far from an angel
Her behaviors and actions had me lose sleep at night
Like an old, dark, creaky house in the movies settling and
Haunting me whether she was near or far away
I was tired of the rumors I had been hearing about her
Running around with other guys
Questioning her, I received no answers and no truth
Vengefully, my rumor became real
I lost my halo and wings
Blemishing my monogamous perfection to her
I'm not sure why I began to break down like I did
Prior to answering the phone
Maybe it was God showing me that whatever happens in the dark
Comes to the light
Maybe it was guilt
Maybe it was the feeling of being caught
Maybe I was fearful of hurting and losing her this way
It could have been the combination of all those things
But as the truth set in
I became nervous and began sweating profusely
I nearly fell to the floor
As what seemed like the Trumpet of God had sounded
and I hadn't prayed to be saved or forgiven
My insides turned like the wringing of soaked towels
Saturated in water
My mouth and throat were completely dry

Like baked riverbeds in the desert
I couldn't speak and tears were streaming down my face
My nose began to run like the Mississippi River into New Orleans
After the levies had broken
She must have known I was home because the phone kept ringing
She used the annoying sound as some sort of GPS or echolocation
After I gathered myself and answered the phone
I pretended not to make out the words she was saying
But somehow, I knew each and every word
No translation was needed
I remember hearing the hurt in her voice
I remember feeling her pain as she cried hysterically
Over what I had allegedly done
I remember wailing like this at a close relative or love one's funeral
I knew then that she really cared about it
I knew then that she really loved me
I knew then that this wasn't just a young girl
Having an upperclassman experience for games and gossip
The sincerity of her emotions brought conviction upon me in a way
I never thought possible
There was no mockery or laughing
And no signs of satisfaction for what I had done to get back at her
I couldn't change what happened, but I understood that
I had to get better and change as a young man

Getting revenge is a double edge sword best kept sheathed, because you never know when the blade will be thrust into you!

She's Not Pregnant*

I received many letters of interest from colleges and universities, but this was my first from a university that I coveted. I went to visit Cornell my junior year and loved it. I was beyond ecstatic. I was ready to go. I wanted to share the news with my parents, but no one was home. I immediately called my girlfriend at the time to tell her the good news. Initially, she was as excited as I was when I asked her, "Guess what? I got a letter of interest from Cornell University, isn't that great?" By the pause in her voice, I knew she wasn't truly happy for me, but I was not going to let her ruin the moment. In fact, she had some news of her own on one of the happiest days in my life.

She says, "I didn't want to tell you, but I'm pregnant!"

All the air went out of me. My head started spinning, and my heart was beating like I just finished running a marathon. A short argument began as I refuted her claim.

I asked, "What do you mean you're pregnant? You can't be because I wore condoms with you every time."

She said, "They are not one hundred percent proof!"

I said, "If you are it can't be mine because we had sex three days ago and prior to that it has been about two weeks. I couldn't finish because your older sister came into the house looking for you. To my knowledge, you can't get pregnant if I didn't bust in you. Plus, I had on a condom."

Like media trying to minimize potential damage I asked, "When did you find out and why didn't you say anything sooner? Did you tell your parents yet?"

She said, "I just found out. I haven't told them yet, but I have to."

I said," I can see their faces now. My mother and father are going to kill me! My mom and dad are going to call your parents after I tell them what you told me."

I asked her once again, "Are you sure you're pregnant?"

She says, "Yes, I'm sure!"

Before I hung up the phone I said, "I'm going to tell them after dinner tonight and see what they say. I'll talk to you later, bye!"

Scared out of my mind
Memories of the previous parent to son conversations
Haunted me
None of which included any babies in my unraveling future
I didn't know what I was going to say,
But it had to be said
I wasn't raised to lie or make excuses

My mother started cooking dinner about 4:30 p.m. and my father just came in the door asking me to call him once dinner was ready. He wanted to jump in the shower, eat and relax after a long day at work. I didn't know how much relaxing either of them was going to do after I give them the news. I wasn't hungry, but I ate just the same. I had this feeling that she wasn't pregnant. I wanted to postpone telling them until I knew for sure. For the first time in a long time, I didn't have much to talk about at the kitchen table. My parents knew something was wrong but couldn't put their fingers on it. They asked me was I feeling okay.

I said, "Yes, I'm stuffed, but I do want to talk to you both after dinner if that's okay?"

They both replied, "Sure!"

I excused myself from the table and went upstairs to make a phone call to my best friend before I relayed the news to my parents. I found increased comfort and confidence after speaking to him about the situation. The moment of truth was in motion as I hung up the phone, ready to face my biggest fear for the night.

Jokingly I said, "Mom and dad would you like to hear the good news or bad news first?"

My dad says, "You can start off with the good news first or whatever you feel comfortable talking about."

My mother says, "Spill it, Christopher!"

I said, "This afternoon I received a letter of interest from Cornell University. I didn't think I could get into an Ivy League School with a 2.8 average."

My father says, "You still have a few semesters to go and if your grades drop you may not be going there at all. Besides, it cost nearly 55,000 per year to go there. We make too much money for you to get financial aid, and you would need a lot of loans to pay for school. If you don't get an academic or sports scholarship for a full ride you may not be able to go because we can't afford 55,000 per year!"

I said, "I will look more into it, but I understand it is expensive." Full of uncertainty I said," Are you ready for the bad news?" I took a deep breath, and said, "My girlfriend told me that she is pregnant, and her parents should be contacting you both sometime soon. Before you say anything, I don't understand how she can be pregnant. We have always used condoms just like you told me to do if the situation arises. I put them on correctly, and I bought them or got them from the clinic in town. There was one time about a month ago that I used one she had in her purse. We never had unprotected sex!"

My mother said, "Christopher, that girl isn't an angel, and she could have poked holes in that condom. I'm not talking bad about her, and she seems nice when she is here, but I've heard so much stuff about her from her family, she's not to be trusted!"

My dad said, "I am not having any grand babies, and you're going to school, and that's that!" If my father did not drive his point home, he says, "If she is pregnant be prepared to get a job because you are paying for the abortion!" Before he got up from the table he says, "We'll talk to her parents and let them know what you said and where we stand! The only way to resolve it is to have her take a pregnancy test."

I said, "Thank you for supporting me. I know it seems bad right now, and you're disappointed in me, but I know she's not pregnant and if she is it's not mine."

What should have been a cordial sit-down
At my girlfriend's home turned into a
Commercial for a heavyweight fight
Two families became uncivil like the blue and gray
Two sets of contenders in close proximity
Both believing their teenagers storyline
Neither set of parents backing down
Verbally jabbing, bobbing and weaving
Trying to get their point across
I didn't call their daughter a ho, but
I told everybody in the room that she's not pregnant
And if she is the baby isn't mine
A preacher and the preacher's wife
Exploded into secular Psalms
The holy became unholy
With their daughter yelling in the background
I am pregnant and it's his child
In opposition, my father bellows
My son is going to college and
He's not having any children
Her parents shouted, she is not having an abortion

We don't believe in that here, we are Christians
Arguing was at its all-time high and
The only thing left to do was to fight!

I didn't know we were all front and center at ringside. There was a crowd forming outside the residence attracted by all the noise. I saw red and blue flashing lights peering through the living room windows. Shortly after there was a loud knock at the front door. Someone called the police to break up the ruckus. We were all asked a few questions by "Wilmington's Finest." My parents and I were escorted to our vehicle without any violence. The daughter came back outside on the porch making smart remarks as we were leaving. She didn't see what was approaching from the south just out of her view. My sister and a few of her girls rolled up five deep with a few other guys in a car behind them. Our family must have had an ally outside in all of the confusion because I didn't have a chance to call anybody. The situation hadn't escalated to that point, but the fire that had been put out started to gain oxygen. The Police Officers that arrived, blocked the entrance to the front porch and ordered everyone to leave with threats of arresting anyone that didn't comply. My sister and her crew of about eight hopped out of their vehicles and approached the porch. They were screaming obscenities and had bad intentions. They didn't come to party that's for sure. I ran over to my sister who was engaged with an officer for stopping the procession. I told her everything was alright, we got it resolved. My mother and father knew each of her friends' names and began shouting for them to stop and that we were all right. After getting their attention for a short moment, I gave instructions, and we all met down at the end of the block. We agreed to meet at my parents for a full debriefing. No charges were filed on either party's behalf. Both families decided to stay away from one another for a few days to let everything cool down. To resolve the situation in question, both families agreed to have one more meeting to reveal the truth of the matter. A pregnancy test will be provided to prove if she is with child and a DNA test will be taken to determine who the father of the child is, if she is truly pregnant!

The day finally came that decided whether I was going to be a working father, student parent or a happy, young Afro-American male escaping entrapment. The doorbell rang and I answered the door. I was cordial to my ex-girlfriend and her parents as I invited them in. My mother was already in the kitchen waiting. I called my father downstairs, and everyone exchanged pleasantries before the main event. I must say that I expected more drama, but I saw mature and concerned parents working toward a peaceful resolution. My ex-girlfriend's mom and my mother each brought a different brand of the pregnancy test. The mothers opened each test at the same time and read the instructions. Each required the instrumentation to be urinated on to get a result. The color pink meant pregnant, and the color blue was negative. My ex-girlfriend's mother went into the kitchen bathroom with the door open to avoid any foul play on her daughter's end. Test one was completed with no change in color. It remained blue. Test two was completed and confirmed the first. In the voice of Maury Povich, deliberately pausing and teasing the crowd before reading the test results, I said, "She is not pregnant!"

Her parents almost simultaneously asked, "Why did you have us believe that you were pregnant?"

Her response was that she lied because she was afraid that I would meet someone at college and break up with her!

In total disbelief, her parents said, "Chris, Mr. and Mrs. Richardson we are sorry we put you through all this!" In total disgust her parents said, "Girl bring your ass on here! Wait until you get home!"

I couldn't believe it! I don't think any of us could believe it, but it happened. I was happy about the outcome, but I was disappointed and hurt because of the lies that were told and everything that I went through. I thanked my parents for supporting and believing in me. They knew I would make mistakes in my life, but nothing like the lies that devastated my trust in females and my plans for a better future.

Before you decide to engage in extracurricular activities talk to your parent(s), family member(s), doctor(s), or peer(s) that you trust. Learn all you can about protecting yourself from pregnancy and diseases. Learn how to use and put on contraceptives. Remember, your first experience could be your worst or last!

Thanks, Coach

Thanks, Coach! You deserve a big hand for being a great leader, teacher, and mentor to all your players and staff; both on and off the court. Thank you for your support and kind words of encouragement. You always seemed to know what to say at the right time. Thank you for your unwavering dedication to one of the best high school programs in the country. The words are touching but so far from the truth. He didn't deserve a place as a high school coach based on many things including his winning percentage which was less than stellar.

Thank you for undermining and spitting on the hard work and dedication I put into returning to the team. I became a better student taking advanced classes to prepare for college and I worked hard to become a top basketball prospect in the state. Despite the pleas of your staff and my teammates that played with me over the summer in basketball camps with the best players in the Tri-State area, I should have made the team easily. You chose otherwise and suffered one of the worst losing seasons in your career. I am truly happy for you, congratulations Coach! During summer workouts, players and coaches from other programs always asked me to come play for their school. Due to the state's transfer rules I would not be eligible to play for a whole year. It was my senior year. I didn't have another year left. What did my patience and loyalty to a Coach and his team get me? Nothing! Coach, despite your differences with my parents, they cared about my future. They stopped me from playing near the end of my junior year so that I could pull up my overall grade point average for college admissions just in case I wasn't offered a scholarship to play basketball. Coach, you seemed not to care about the team's overall performance in education, just the players you focused on. Despite my dedication and patience to play within your system I never would have seen the light of day because I was a freshman or a sophomore. In your eyes I was too young to be a starter, inexperienced or wet behind the ears.
I wasn't 6'8" and I was an unknown to the public eye. Coach, you chose to move me up in the lineup to fill in spaces when two of

your big men got hurt and one became sick and couldn't return to the team. I believe I should have been starting all along. I guess I should have been happy. Some would say that is the natural order of things, but he previously put me in at garbage time or when the games didn't matter. For the short period I was in the game coaches and players from other teams took notice of me and gave me praise afterward. Something you didn't see or do. I had more heart, and I was better than most of the big men in your starting lineup. I was faster, more athletic, played great defense, a good post game and I had a jump shot. I rarely got a chance to show it. I didn't mind setting hard picks, fouling, rebounding, and doing the dirty work. I had tenacity and toughness, something your team never had outside of a few players. There were many student-athletes on the team who took basic classes, never met a two-point zero average, and never went to class. Somehow, they managed to stay and play on the team. Preferential treatment perhaps, but I saw none of that!

I wore the number twenty-nine. It amazed me how my stats after each game never matched what I contributed on the court. I thought I was crazy at first! Maybe I didn't score five baskets, make three out of five from the free throw line, have four assists, grab six rebounds, four steals and four blocks. After seeing multiple discrepancies between stat keepers at the end of games on player stats and the final box score reported to the newspaper, I knew something wasn't quite right. My aunt came to one of my games and joked with me one night.

She said, "I watched the whole game and I thought you scored eleven points by my count."

I said, "Me too."

The next day the local newspaper reported that I scored five points. I didn't understand how or why my stats were being reported incorrectly, given to the other players, or not being reported at all.

Am I speculating? Was it preferential player treatment or padding player stats? I don't know how it happened or what to think but it happened. No explanation was given by Coach as to why this was happening.

Coach, I didn't learn much from you except X's and O's on a clipboard, names of plays and how they are run. The rest came from watching the NBA, NCAA, playing organized and street basketball outside of school. Coach, I couldn't believe you refused to meet with my parents and me to discuss why I wasn't on the team my senior year. He sent the Assistant Coach to talk to me during school hours to discuss the matter without my parents.

The Assistant Coach said, "On his behalf and the team I should be playing with them, but it's not his decision or the team."

I asked, "Why?"

He told me to talk to the Coach. Coach is still mad at my parents because they took me off the team when he needed me to play. Coach never met with me or my parents on his own merit. I took it upon myself to meet with him and ask him why my name wasn't on the roster my senior season. I caught him walking in the school gym twenty minutes before the team practice. He knew why I was there. He had no place to run or hide. His face turned red when I asked him why?

He said, "I couldn't trust you to be there for the team or keep up with your schoolwork. You left the team when I needed you most and the team needed you."

His decision wasn't based on business, forgiveness, or logic. It was a personal grudge. A grudge that impacted my future. The inner king came out and I replied, "You didn't play me or need me from a freshman to most of my junior year, rotting at the end of the bench. You said, I would have my chance!"

He replied, "Other players needed playing time to be seen by college scouts." As if I didn't need to be evaluated on the same basis!

I said, "What you're telling me doesn't make sense!" Then I blurted, "Three players on the team who couldn't return due to injury or illness around the same time that I was pulled from the team are on the roster this year. Obviously, you didn't hold a grudge against them or say I can't trust you to play on the team because you can't stay healthy!" Trying to reason with him I said, "Four seniors have graduated, and three of the five starters didn't meet a two-point zero average. They played for you last year Coach! How can it be that I cannot play based on something that happened the prior season and I wasn't academically ineligible?" Filled with hurt and anger, I said, "You're not God, and you're not perfect! Put yourself in our shoes as a young man and his parents." As a tear of frustration streamed down my right eye I said, "I am here ready to play! I'm in the best shape of my life with several tutors available to help me in my advanced classes this year and your answer is still no!" I was beyond furious! I slammed both fists into the white cinderblock walls in his office. I wanted to whip his ass something terrible, but that wouldn't have gotten me anywhere except a trip to jail and worse. The consequences were too severe. I wished there was a way I could have transferred to another school in the conference and played against his team twice a year. I would have made Coach pay for his decision and show him how good I've become. I imagined I wouldn't even shake his hand after the game. I would stare him in the eyes and smile as I walk by relishing in our victory.

Thanks, Coach, for snatching my opportunity as a senior to showcase my growth and talent as a basketball player. Thank you for crushing my dream of being recruited on a basketball scholarship to play ball at a major university. Coaches like you are the reason why so many student athletes go unnoticed or don't play beyond high school because it's about you and who you want to flourish in your environment. As a coach you affect the lives of so many young men and women. There is a fine line between enriching, hindering, and destroying the dreams of those looking up to you. Under your instruction, your influence and power are immense. It's something you didn't quite understand or maybe you did and just didn't care. Thanks Coach!

Kim

When you left this earth
I felt you were taken too soon
Your passing left a void in my chest
A hollowed cavity with nothing in it
Except the sorrow, pain and guilt that cemented my heart
I honestly felt and believed that I failed you and the family
I was your brother and protector
I wasn't there to protect and help you when you needed me the most
Especially from that controlling, abusive, and
Bullshit ass nigga you were with
I was in college at the time but that is no excuse
I blamed myself for your death and
For many years I carried that burden
Like I weighed three thousand pounds
When you were lowered into the ground, I changed
The sorrow, guilt, and pain became anger
I was angry at God
I was angry at that nigga
I was mad at the world
I became everything I was taught not to be and
I embraced it
I liked its empowering flavor in my heart and soul
For years, the world has been prompting me to become an ass
Like kids begging please, pretty please!
I gave in and the world got what it had asked for, an asshole
I vowed to give one hundred percent to any
And everything I set my mind to do
But not in the way you think
I vowed to smite anyone who tried to hurt
Or take advantage of me
I promised not to become a statistic to anyone
But make someone else become a statistic by my hands
I vowed revenge on the fuck boy

Who assisted death in taking you away too soon
It took me years to let it all go
Karma will handle my light work
But I truly love and miss you dearly sis

Death is as certain as life itself. When it happens to the ones we love, it hurts and changes our lives and perceptions forever. We must learn to deal with our pain and perception in a positive and constructive way. Using drugs, hurting others, and indulging in negative behaviors won't bring them back. Know that your loved ones are always with you and watching over you every day. It is okay to feel sad or miss them, but they also want you to be happy and lead great lives in their physical absence.

Tested*

My family and I just buried my sister. I followed the university's policy for bereavement. I was only gone one week. Although my heart was heavy like someone placed a mountain on my chest, I was ready to go back to school and get back in the mix of things. I knew in my heart that this was what my sister wanted me to do. I was highly motivated and upon my return to school I immediately went to all of my instructors to get all the assignments and information that I may have missed in a week. I made every effort to be like Heinz and catch up, but why did I have to come back to circumstances that hit me literally and figuratively right after a tragedy? It was too soon to be tested or played with, not like this. What would you do if you came back to school and the university and instructor you trusted with your education didn't have your best interest in mind? What would you do if you were forced to take a test that you were not aware of or prepared for?

The chemistry professor had put in for family leave to take care his ailing brother. The classes under his instruction were suspended until he came back, or another professor was hired to take his place. He had to submit grades for all his students before he was able to take leave. Regardless of anyone else's situation, he made haste and waste of any student in the way of his plans. Upon entering the Science Facility to see the Chemistry Professor, I was shocked to learn of his situation through other students. I didn't know how this was going to affect me, but I was about to find out. Once I entered the classroom, he waived me to the front of the class and told me I had to take an exam based on the last five chapters of the book. I had visualized all I needed was two or three hours to study the material so that I would not fail the exam. He told me I needed to take the test now or fail. I advised him of my situation. I avidly requested that I review the material next to him on the floor, in his office or in the hall outside of class and then take the test. His answer was still no.

If my patience and understanding was a receding hair line
I went bald or purposely shaved my head
I wished to test his jaw with force
As I was forced to take the exam
It took everything in me to digress
And not make a mess of this situation
It didn't take a rocket scientist to figure out I failed the test

He was rude and unreasonable to me. I felt disrespected and cheated. I felt my rights as a student had been violated. On the way out of the classroom I crumpled the results of the test and handed it to him. I advised him that this was far from over. The next time you see me it will be before the School Board. We will see what they have to say about it. I was unwavering and determined to make sure that mediation took place despite some resistance from the administration. Who were they to minimize my complaint as a student? I wasn't going to let him leave and give me a grade that would cripple my ability to get into a graduate program and diminish my hopes of getting a job in my field of study. My family and I didn't have the money to repeat any classes. The day finally came, and I made my case in front of the University Board. I said what I needed to say, and the instructor did as well. I was confident the Board would rule in my favor. I didn't get into any trouble at school. I got decent grades. I worked part-time to pay the remaining balance of my tuition. Eleven days ago, I experienced a sudden and unfortunate circumstance in my life. Who would rule against that? The Board convened for a short recess and returned. I appeared to be relaxed, but I was anxious and awaited their decision.

The group's appointee stated, "As members of the Board, we support our students just as we support our staff. It is our duty to settle disputes in all fairness based on the facts and testimonies within policy. With that said, we have heard each of your testimonies and we have the upmost confidence in the instructor to make the right decision. We will support his decision on the matter, and it will be final. Professor, what is your decision based on the circumstances and facts presented today?" I could have sworn they were supposed to make the decision on the matter, not him. A couple of seconds seemed like a lifetime as I watched his lips form a word that began with an unpleasant bold consonant. The sound "N" resonated from his lips and ended in "O." I didn't hear anything else he said after that. Like Bernie, the university and instructor Madoff with the last bolt that held my universe intact. I got up out of my chair and slammed my fists on the table. I looked at the Board and then turned to him and I said, "That's it, your answer is no! You all are allowing him to do this to me! Mess up my grade for this class and my future?"

The appointee responded, "We are sorry Mr. Allen, the decision has been made!"

Livid I yelled, "The decision has been made?"

Like weapons are being tested, I went ballistic! I turned over a table or two and tossed a few chairs in disgust. Luckily, no one moved or approached me because things would have gotten really ugly.

I shouted, "Nothing good will happen in any of your lives. I hope you all get sick and die of something extremely painful!"

Before I totally lost it, I walked backwards out the conference room with my back toward the exit. Angry, frustrated, and hurt tears began to fall from my eyes. I watched as their faces began to ease of fear and mortification. I knew what was going to happen next, so I went to my dorm room and began packing my things. I got a call from a friend that worked for the Campus Security. He told me before they called the State Police that he had talked to the President and the Board and vouched that no further action would take place on my end. The University wanted to resolve the matter quietly without any further incident. I told my friend what had happened and that I would withdraw from school rather than be expelled. Either way, I was being made to leave just as I was forced to take the test. The Security Officer walked me over to the Admissions Office so that I could sign the necessary paperwork to withdraw from school. I advised him that I didn't want to speak to the President, the Board, or the instructor to keep the peace. If the decision was not going to be overturned and no apology was going to be made on their end there would be no point in having a conversation. It was Wednesday and I had until the end of the week to leave campus. I called my parents and let them know what happened. Before the evening was out my ride came and I headed home trying to wrap my mind around what just happened.

The foundations I was taught to trust and believe in meant nothing to me anymore. My faith in God, people and the education system had been totally lost. My bottom gave way mentally and emotionally as I plummeted into depression and darkness. I embraced my pain and misfortune and transformed into something new. Like the singer Bill Withers' song, "Ain't No Sunshine" where he's gone.

Life is not fair, and life will test you! It's about how you respond to these challenges that make you great, resilient or not. You will not be seen or judged by what happened or what someone did to you. You will be seen and judged by how you respond to the situation!

What could the administration and board have done differently to address the situation? What could I have done differently to address this issue?

CHAPTER 2

My Vice

My vice became my strength, crutch, ally, and weakness
It deadened the exploding landmines and turbulence
That shook me from within,
It fought off the crippling effects of depression with a depressant
Crushed by landslides of disappointments and pain
I became a slave to a liquid that drowned out my perceived reality
In the form of bliss
Every day I repeated the same cycle
With the precision of an atomic watch
Filling my void with my vice

It is important to deal with your personal issues constructively without using any vices! Masking is an invitation to addiction! Addiction is like a roach infestation, once it has a hold of your house (your temple) it is almost impossible to get it rid of it! IF YOU CAN HELP IT DON'T START USING VICES!

My Special Friend

No matter what she did I didn't have to worry about anyone else
She proved her loyalty to me
I never had to make a call to go see her
I could go get her whenever I wanted
She allowed me to touch her and taste her anytime I wanted
She gave me headshots and
Never asked for the act to be reciprocated
Many days she put me to sleep and never left me alone
She watched over me like an angel
As I slept peacefully in her warm embrace
I could always count on her to be there
Whether I was in a good mood, a bad mood
Or just going through some things
She knew exactly how to cheer me up and
Take my mind off whatever was bothering me
I was only seeing her out of convenience
I thought I was in total control of our relationship, but
She rendered me defenseless without a fight
I didn't know what we had would become so serious
But now that we are here
I surrendered to my special friend
In the tall clear or colored bottle

My Woman's Gone

She was devoted to me like the Mayans to the Sun
She became a little jealous
When I spent too much time away from her
Working or tending to my obligations
But she was never far from my mind
Like a person that you're highly attracted too, admire, or just met
I found myself going out of my way to be with her
Even if it meant calling off work the next day
Hanging out all night, spending rent or
Bill money on her just to have a good time
She'd whisper softly in my left ear
Don't worry darling, you'll make it up working overtime
I didn't know if I was spoiling her or if she was spoiling me
But everything began to spoil as a result of our union
I couldn't believe I didn't see it sooner
She was so selfish and jealous
It was all about her
If she couldn't have me to herself nobody could have me
She didn't care that I had family, children, bills, or friends
She manipulated and controlled me mentally, emotionally and
Physically, like a puppet on strings
My finances and life began to crumble and
Bow like untreated wood in extreme weather
I needed time away from this toxic love relationship
I made up my mind to leave her altogether
One day we were good
The next day I'm cursing her out because unknowingly
I spent all my money on her
She practically lives with me and doesn't contribute a damn dime
Towards any utilities, gas, rent or food
She didn't work or have any desire to do so
Why would I agree to be a part of this madness?
Even after the breakup
She didn't respect it or take our boundaries seriously
She kept showing up everywhere I used to hang out
Embarrassing me in public
Screaming and demanding
That our relationship wasn't over until she says it's over

She even tried making me jealous by staring at me
Then flirting with other men and women
As the bartender poured her into their glasses
She positioned her hips spread eagle at the top of their glasses
Electrifying their lips and palates with her flavorful essence
That night I was truly done with her
How could she play with my head and emotions like that?
She was trying to reel me back in
Like a large fish hooked on high-poundage test line
If I were a weaker man
I would have taken her offer of indulgence for the night
We broke up many times before and I went back to her
Many days I felt really bad and simply miserable without her
It was the best decision for me, I mean us
We still speak, and I see her from time to time
But nothing like it used to be
I have no need or connection to her now
I have a new woman in my life
Her name is Sobriety
I lost her too because I couldn't keep myself from
Picking up other's like my ex in her presence

Grown and Opinionated

Now that I am eighteen and grown
I can say what I want to say
To whomever I want to say it to
Whenever I want to say it and how I want to say it
No apologies!
But it is amazing how one look, word, or opinion in a conversation
Can turn a perfect afternoon or evening into a total disaster
Respect and tolerance of another's opinion or words
Other than my own wasn't my strong suit
I didn't care who I talked to or argued with
Just know that I am right!
Your thoughts or feelings about me or what I said didn't matter!
It's my opinion and I am grown!

You have the right to your opinion, thoughts, and feelings, but it is no excuse to be ugly, rude, or disrespectful to anyone!
The keys to being grown and mature are being respectful and understanding of other's thoughts, and opinions!

Caught Up

I got started in the game because I was broke
I just had my first child and
A full-time job couldn't come fast enough
A minimum wage job didn't pay enough
I needed money to go back to college
I wanted an apartment and a nice car to drive
Fresh clothes, new kicks, book money, groceries
A matching 14k Cuban gold link, bracelet, and ring
Caught up
I was afraid of going to prison
But the need to survive, my dreams, and curing my financial woes
Erased that fear and turned it into caution
As I began to make money it poisoned my fingertips
Like ink from retail receipts going straight into my veins
The more money I made the more I spent
I totally lost all sensibility of money management
I could care less about a rainy day or going back to college
I can make back what I spent today on tomorrow
Caught up
It wasn't that I couldn't attract women on my own
But the lifestyle was a female magnet
Luring all types of women
Different ethnicities, hood, church and professional
I was my own boss
I could get up anytime I wanted
Work as long as I wanted
I could damn near get anything I wanted
Hanging with my crew at parties and clubs
The money and the attention
It became highly addictive like what I was selling
I was admired
I felt like a big man
I felt important in my hood, and I loved it
My vision of going back to school
Faded like images in my peripheral vision
Forgotten like thoughts or dreams that I never wrote down
I was caught up in a seemingly beautiful web like Charlotte's
And I couldn't break free

I honestly don't know if I wanted to stop
I didn't control the game anymore
It controlled me
Like a mannequin on puppet strings
I was caught up by the allure of the streets and money

We all want to be liked, accepted, and appreciated. We all want to have nice things. Everything has a cost or price. Are you willing to make the positive sacrifices to legally get what you want or are you willing to compromise your character, your freedom, your present, your future, your family and your friends to obtain money and material things illegally? Illegal life, fast money, men, women, jewelry and clothes have value in the streets, but it diminishes the value of your life, character and soul! Do your best not to get caught up!

I Used to Be Him

I used to be him
That immature, ignorant
No job or minimal job complacent
Always complaining
24 -7, block hanging, drug trafficking, coke slinging
Alcohol drinking,
If I could, I would hit four ladies a day coochie banging
Slouched over, spoke illiterate
Best believe, if you started it, I would finish it

I used to be him
That non-law abiding
Fuck the police hollering was my motto
If I felt you were trying to disrespect me
I would plot and lay you down like tile ho
I was a Gahd amongst many Gahds
So, sniff, take a whiff
You couldn't tell me nothing I knew I was the shit

I used to be him
Gossip collabin'
Talked about what I got bragging
Quick to swing on any man and
Everything I did was someone else's fault except for my own

I used to be him
That conceited and obnoxious
Everyone's below me abusive talking
If you weren't getting money with me
Or if her panties weren't dropping
You meant nothing to me, or we weren't talking

I used to be him
The man who had no fear of death
Walked around like money and respect was a bullet proof vest
Attitude was the most effective demeanor on set
I done many things that invited my last breath
Friend or foe I cursed a mile a sec

I've robbed and been robbed so who's really doing the theft
I was a sorry excuse for a man and behaved much less

I used to be him
The man that kept my father up half the night
Comforting my mother
Because she couldn't sleep peacefully, tossing and turning
In and out of bed, pacing the floor many nights
Worrying, crying, praying, wondering if her son was safe
Dreading the fact that at any time
She could receive that phone call day or night
Not to get her son out of jail or prison but
Taking that ride to the coroner's office to identify her son's body
Preparing him for his final resting place
She had already lost a daughter, but to lose a son to nonsense
Just didn't make sense

I used to be him
I will never teach another to be like him
Society accepts, glorifies, and breeds him
If I could go back and change who I was and what I've done
I wouldn't be him
There would be no trace of him
There is no place for him in anyone's lives
Not now or ever
I used to be him

Divine Intervention I

My younger brother and his friends from Glasgow High School were walking outside of the White House during their field trip to Washington DC when a Caucasian woman dressed in gypsy like clothing began walking toward the group. Out of all the young men, she zeroed in and stopped to talk to my brother. He told me she had a strange accent and then began to convey this incredible message. She said, "You don't know me, and I don't know you, but I need you to pay attention and listen very carefully. You have several male figures in your life that are important to you. One is a father figure, and the other two may be your brother or uncle. The one I'm speaking of may be a brother and I feel he is very close to you. Whatever he is doing produces a lot of money. It may be legal or illegal, but he is in danger and needs to stop what he is doing and walk away now. In my vision I see him sitting on a park bench covered in roses. There are snakes around the bench and his feet. This means that people he considers to be close to him want to harm him. He needs to leave them alone or get away from them because he will defend himself and risk his life and freedom in doing so. He will also have a court date plus or minus two or three days before or after November 23rd. He will get off this time and avoid jail time, but if he continues to do what he is doing, he will not be so lucky the next time."

Divine intervention can be delivered in many ways if you are open to receive the message. This message was well received, and I took appropriate actions to stay out of trouble to extend my life experiences. Please do the same!

Divine Intervention II*

I used a cheap track phone from another state to call my contact and place my order before heading to New York, otherwise known as "The City". My supply was low, and I was eager to go and get back as soon as possible. Once I got the call back to confirm the price, amount, and day, I prepared my ensemble of two disguises, and I was ready to travel north. One for the trip up and one for the journey back. There was an increase in cars with out of state tags being pulled over leaving *the city*, so I precisely timed my trip down to the second with the compliance of public transportation. A system that seemed not to be in my favor, so I thought.

The train to *the city* was over an hour late. My two eyebrows became a unified frown as my schedule and patience was shot at point blank range. The first of the month was less than 18 hours away.

> *Time is money and money is time*
> *Neither can be mine*
> *If I miss the grind with no supply!*

My instincts and eyes were peeled to spot the plain clothes on duty as well as those in uniform. I casually avoided any interaction with them during and after the wait for the train. Fifteen thousand dollars is a lot to lose and recover if the Police got their hands on it. I didn't want to be questioned like Socrates or be tied up in miles of red tape trying to get the money back. As the train arrived, I quickly pulled out my track phone and called the supplier letting him know I was on my way in code.
There was no response from him which was odd. When I reached Philly, then Jersey, I did the same, and there was still no response. I knew then that something wasn't quite right as I got a sick feeling in the pit of my stomach. I couldn't turn back now. The supply was needed, and I wasn't trying to lose any money or go back empty handed, so I pressed on. When I arrived in *the city* almost two hours past my original schedule, I weaved my way through the many patrons of the public transportation system. I was in a sea of multi-cultural people that may not have even

noticed my presence as I made my way outside to catch a cab to my destination. I was delayed yet again due to an accident on the expressway and my time between being ready for the first of the month was less than thirteen hours away. Inch by inch the cab driver made his way past the bottleneck in traffic and hit a fissure. The driver wasted no time accelerating to my destination. I kept staring at the meter because it rose to an amount I didn't want to pay. Upon nearing my destination on Saint Nick, I asked the cab driver to keep driving. The avenue was normally filled with a plethora of people and rhythmic music. It was a ghost town. It was eerie and unsettling to see. I asked the driver to pull over on another block and wait for me. He kept the meter running and I gave him my limited-edition Fossil Watch to hold until I got back. Dressed in street clothes I grabbed my carry bag and jumped out the cab. I began walking quickly to my destination. As I reached the building and walked inside, I kept my eyes peeled for possible jackers, police or anything keeping me from my long-awaited prize in white gold. I was met with echoes from my own footsteps and cloaked images of past visitations. There was a sign in English and Spanish on the elevator doors stating it was out of order. I was in good shape so running up eight flights of stairs wasn't a problem, but there was no air-conditioning. I was met with the open hand of June's summer heat trapped in a large apartment building. As I proceeded up the steps the usual hustle and bustle of occupants going up and down the stairs didn't exist. I saw an older Spanish man making his way down the steps from the sixth floor and I asked him in my best Espanola, "Donde esta todo el mundo? Paso algo?"

I believe he told me that four people on the eighth floor were killed.

I said, "Gracias," and proceeded up the stairs as the hair on my neck began to stand up. I knew something was wrong! I couldn't believe what I saw. The apartment I needed to go to was blocked off with yellow caution tape. It was a crime scene. My heart began pounding with anxiety trying to figure out my next move. I felt bad for my connect and those that were with him. My instinct was to turn around and walk the other way, but my curiosity to see what was on the other side of the taped door took over. No one was around so I pulled the tape off the entrance, and I pushed the door open. I was in awe of the dried blood on several room floors, the number of bullet holes in the walls, and the knife wounds in the couch seats. I didn't need to see anything else. My curiosity was fulfilled. I knew what happened to them. My supplier had been murdered for drugs, money, or some other deed unknown to me. It was clear that if I had come the previous day or sooner, I may have been caught in the middle of this tragedy. I could have been arrested, kidnapped, robbed, tortured, or killed. I was truly thankful for the delay that morning and the days before. I rushed down the steps and out the building to find the cab waiting in the next block. I didn't know any other supplier, but I took my chances on meeting a new connect between 189th and 125th streets. I wasn't out of the woods yet, but I knew the delay was divine intervention.

Divine Intervention III

Unnerved by the previous trip to New York, things just didn't feel the same anymore. The allure wasn't there. The veil over my eyes was lifting. I didn't have the heart or the stomach for this shit anymore! I knew God was warning me to stop and I had a choice to make. Either pay the local convenience prices to get mostly shake, walk away scot-free, or go back *up top* to purchase pure white to make a hefty profit and satisfy my customers one last time. The warning signs were all around me, but greed and obligations were my motivating factor. It was getting too tough to maintain the lifestyle, remain human and not violate my temporary probation. Three months is a long time to avoid a possible felony assault charge when people were provoking me left and right. I had an image and a reputation to protect. I wasn't a gangster, but I could hold my own if I was tested. My assault and weapons charges were pending, and I had to stay out of trouble until after my court date. I was blessed to save for a rainy day and damn it, the rain came.

I almost got shot after a fight over an eighty-dollar sale from one of my customers. If I hadn't arrived a few seconds earlier, the incident might not have taken place. A new young face wanted to argue and fight over a customer and sale that wasn't his to begin with. After trouncing the young man, he got up off the ground ran toward a brown paper bag near an alley and pulled out a gun. As he took aim at me the gun clicked repeatedly, but it didn't fire. I couldn't let this go. Outraged and furious, I chased him about ten blocks to no avail. Maybe it was divine intervention that allowed him to escape his fate as he ran blindly into swiftly moving traffic without getting hit. I was angry, but I wasn't that crazy to follow him in that traffic. I warned him that I'd better not ever see him out on the block again or I was going to kill him. Later that day, a user I thought was my peoples or at least neutral, tried to get me to sell drugs to an Undercover Cop. The deal that was being offered was too good to be true. It just didn't make sense mathematically from ordinary day to day sales. Fifteen dime bags of cocaine for two-hundred and fifty dollars? I'm too smart for that. Another dealer thought he was getting over. He took the sale and was arrested shortly after. Early the next morning I had to approach a group of young thugs. I made them apologize to my young boy for jumping him, taking his money and package. It was all given back to me, but I had to make an example of their Lieutenant in charge. He probably gave the order to have it done and it happened on his watch. I assaulted him with a pistol and chased him off the block. It was my only recourse. I couldn't shoot him with a crowd full of witnesses. That would have been terrible for my court case let alone my future. With the amount of snitching going on I would have gotten ten or more years without blinking. Later that day the Wilmington Task Force ran up in a house I was selling out of on Bennet Street and thankfully, I was able to escape. I climbed through a second-story window onto a small ledge giving me a chance to pull myself up on the rooftop and run across a block of row houses. I made my way down a broken fire escape, through an alley and sprinted my way to freedom. I knew this was karma for what I did earlier that day. I knew God was warning me. I knew God was making every effort to break me free of the web I wove seven years ago. I started to see and feel the oppression and harm I was doing to my community and those around me. I knew I wasn't supposed to go to *the city*, but I decided to make one last trip. One last hurrah before I gave up the life! I had no problems getting to *the city* and purchasing what I came after. With five hundred and fifty plus grams of coke placed in six plastic zip lock bags, each wrapped in black electrical tape to obscure the smell, I carefully strapped them to my waist and crotch with electrical tape. I put on my suit and tie; grabbed my travel bag and I was ready to head home. The plan started to fall apart after I flagged down and got into an illegal black cab. A fake cab! How was I supposed to know? Like a racial slur, they all looked the same to me. I didn't get two city blocks from where I was picked up before I heard the *Whoop, Whoop!* The red, white, and blue lights I dreaded to see ricocheted like bullets inside the vehicle, tearing my body apart with utter shock and fear. My luck had run out. I knew I was done. They must have made me or had my connect under surveillance. I took one too many chances gambling with my life for money. My heart pounded with fear as my mind began racing on how I was going to escape this one-way trip to a local precinct, then Riker's Island. I thought about removing the packages and placing them into my travel bag that had my name, address, and phone number on it. As if this was a truly brilliant idea! I was sitting in the right rear passenger seat of the cab, and I didn't want to raise any suspicion to what I was holding. I didn't make any sudden movements as both officers closed their vehicle doors and came up on both sides of the black cab. One police officer tapped on the cab drivers window and advised him on why he was stopped and then asked him for his license, registration, and some other documents. They didn't stop him because I was trafficking; the driver didn't have the proper licensing or visual stickers needed to operate his vehicle. I didn't know how they saw it and I didn't care. There was a chance I could walk away from this! The other officer noticed that I was clean cut, wearing a suit and tie. I was asked for my name, ID, and where was I headed. He also asked if I had weapons or anything illegal on me. I told him my name, gave him my college ID, and stated that I was an intern on my way to work downtown. I told him that I had nothing illegal or any weapons on me. He gave me back my ID and told me to sit tight as he walked back to the police vehicle. My chance came to rid myself of this heavy burden. My survival instincts kicked in and all I could think about was the quote, "Better him than me!" I quickly removed the six packages with subtle movements and tossed them in the rear floor behind the cab driver. I used my left foot to push the remaining visible packages firmly underneath the driver's seat just in case they decided to search me or the vehicle. I would be free of any wrongdoing, so I hoped. I would be out of a lot of product and money, but I would have my life and freedom to recoup what I lost.

The officer I spoke to first, came back, opened the door, and asked, "Did you know you were in an illegal cab?"

I said, "No, I was running behind this afternoon and needed to get downtown. The subway would have taken me five blocks out of the way. I'm terribly late!"

The officer said, "Your name came back clear and you're free to go."

Before I completely got out of the cab, I asked the officer if I could I get my change and a cell phone that dropped on the floor behind driver's rear side.

He replied, "Go ahead."

I was glad he was a flirt and a girl watcher. His attention was diverted toward three fine Hispanic women walking by with curves for days. I threw my bag on the floor behind the driver's seat. I leaned over, reaching under the seat, and recovered the six packages.

I quickly put them in the travel bag just as the officer asked me if I had gotten everything.

I replied," Yes."

I stepped out of the cab and proceeded to walk three city blocks behind three heavenly bodies before getting into a yellow taxicab this time. I knew this was God. I knew this was divine intervention, but it wasn't over yet. I still had to get home. After I had given the cab driver my destination I was in a different world. I was thanking God repeatedly over and over again! The elation I felt to get out of that jam was like nothing I had ever felt before. Time seemed to stand still. I didn't realize I had reached Penn Station so quickly. The cab driver started knocking on the plexiglas rambling about the fare. I paid the driver and proceeded inside to get my train ticket back to Wilmington, Delaware. Upon standing in line, I looked up and saw that I had 10 minutes before the train departed for home. There was a sizable line, but it dwindled quickly. I ran as if I were being chased by wild dogs. I made it to the train with two minutes to spare. With the week I had, it was the first time I slept peacefully in months. I clutched my bag as if my hands were a part of the leather. I woke up just in time to hear the Conductor stating the next stop was the Wilmington Train Station. My eyes quickly focused as I saw countless police cars and emergency vehicles flashing white, red, and blue lights in front of the train station. My first thought was that a terrible accident had occurred nearby. The closer the train moved toward the station I looked out of my window and saw Detectives and Police Officers with dogs all over the plat form.

I said to myself, "Oh my God, it can't be!"

I was trying to figure out who I pissed off and if I told anyone I was making this trip for the police to be tipped off. I was certain I didn't say anything to anyone. I couldn't get off the train right away because there was a line standing up gathering their belongings. The Conductor didn't allow anyone to leave the car once it stopped. I took the address tag off my bag and placed it on the floor.
I began to slide my bag underneath someone else's seat hoping to be out of harm's way if I was taken in for interrogation. The Wilmington Task Force and other law enforcement personnel walked thru each train checking person after person trying to find a match of a photo. It seemed like the process was taking forever but it was still too soon for all intent and purposes. The car door opened, and I swore I swallowed my heart. I began to sweat like I was walking in the Sahara Desert. Maybe it was just my time as I relinquished all hope and sat back to accept my fate. I was about ten rows back on the left side of the train. I saw a detective and a task force member stop in front of a man sitting in the third row on the right side of the train. They asked him his for name and ID. Once he responded they told the young man he needed to come with them. They grabbed his luggage and escorted him off the train in hand cuffs without incident. I don't remember them quoting the Miranda Rights, but I was so relieved to see they were not looking for me that I could have screamed. I had to keep my cool and gather my wits because it was far from over. Detectives, Police and the K-9's were still on the platform. If the dogs got a whiff of what I was carrying I was done. I gathered all my things as the Conductor had gotten permission to allow the riders to leave the train. A nice older couple allowed me to get in front of them to exit the train. I walked and talked with them until I got past the first wave of blue suits. There was a second wave along the commuter ramp still chatting about the arrest. Along the ramp I saw a set of steps that led to a walkway that would take me out of harm's way and directly to the parking deck. It was worth the walk to escape capture. Once I cleared the parking deck, I immediately got in a small line to wait for yet another cab. The next cab pulled up, and the driver got out asking if I needed help with putting my belongings in the trunk. A hand touched my shoulder, and a strong masculine voice said, "Is the suitcase behind you yours?"

I turned around to address the man that touched me. I was in pure shock. It was a police officer. He had a female officer with him as well.

I said, "No, it's not mine," and quickly got into the cab.

When the driver pulled off, I gave a flirty smile and waved bye to the female officer. After giving the driver my destination, the whole day flashed before me. I thought about how lucky I was to survive the day and the prior two weeks intact. I could have been in the hospital, dead in an abandoned building, the woods, a river, jail, or prison. So many things crossed my mind. I thought about my children not having their father around and who would be raising them. I knew I had to get it together and get out of this life on the streets. I was thankful for the divine intervention and that I had another chance to get my life right.

The street life is nothing to glorify or play with! Too many men and women have gambled with their lives and freedom to live this lifestyle and crapped out! When I say that you stand to lose everything, I do mean everything! Think about who and what you will lose when you get jammed up?

It's All Good

It's all good when you're on the streets making that money
Everybody knows your face and name like a celebrity on TV
Everybody wants to be down with you
Everybody wants to smoke, drink, and party with you
Everybody wants something from you
But when the beef starts, and problems arise
Those with your hands out, where you all at?
But it's all good!

The women about that life want to be seen with you
Do whatever it takes to be down with you
They say we'll stand by you
But when the money gets low
Or you have to do the time for the crimes
Where the hell you ladies at?
But it's all good!

In my experience, if I didn't have an attorney
He or she was court appointed
Appointing your ass straight to jail then prison
Nobody reached out, visited, or wrote anymore
Nobody accepted my collect calls or put money on my books
But it's all good!

It hurt when you have protected and
Helped others keep their lights on
Pay phone bills, car notes, rent, and put food in their homes
In a blink of an eye, they all abandon you
But it's all good!

The people you think would stand by you
Are the first to break into your home and
Take your personal items like TV's, money, furniture, and clothes
They'll let your apartment; home or car get repossessed
But when I was out
They all pledged loyalty and support
But it's all good!

It is really funny how people change when your situation changes. Especially, when your situation no longer benefits them
But it's all good!

The street life is very enticing. The void or fulfillment that you may be seeking won't be found in the streets. What you will find are manipulators, liars, opportunist, addicts, and more opportunities to fill jails, prisons, and graveyards!

My Money

Money is something we wish we had all the time
Lots of it like good friends and family
I thought you was my mans, my money
My bro, bro-ham, my people, my boy, my ace
Most importantly my friend
I trusted and believed in you wholeheartedly
I thought I could count on you
I believed in a friend's loyalty to the end
Over anything even money and women
I thought you was my man's my money

Who had your back at the club ready to tear shit up
When niggas wanted to beef over a woman
That wasn't even theirs to claim?
When things got rough, and you didn't have a stable place to live
Who immediately went out and got the down payment
And first months' rent for a townhouse as roommates?
Even when I knew I would not get the money back that you
Borrowed, I still went out on a limb to help you
When have you done that for me?
When you had no transportation
I would let you drive my car while I was at work
So that you could look for a job and do what you had to do
But when you got your car
I couldn't drive yours under any circumstances
There were times my car broke down when you were driving it
I got it fixed and never asked you for a dime
Nor did you offer any assistance or recoupment
Whether my car was at a full tank, half a tank or a quarter tank
You never brought the car back where the gas hand needed to be
I thought I could share anything with you Money
I believed it would never get back to me in a twisted way
But I was wrong
No matter what happened between us I always had your back
It didn't matter what people said about you
Or what you said about me
No matter what we said to each other
And no matter what I saw in your actions, I dismissed it

I forgave you
I chose to see the good in you and
Not who you really were as a person
The love, friendship and
Loyalty I've extended to you has not been reciprocated
Some things take a long time to see and accept
But now that my eyes are open
You never agreed to do anything
That wasn't advantageous to yourself
I can see and smell the fickleness coming out of your pores
It's a shame that I feel and see you differently
You still cool with me, but it will be a long time
Before you earn back the friendship that you lost

Be careful of who you call a friends because they may not be a friend at all; they are the benefactors of the friendship, not your friend!

To Prove a Point

Remember when I told you bruh
Watch the company you keep
Where you lay your head and where you sleep
It wasn't me, but it inadvertently became me for proving a point
When I told you she hit on me
I showed you the piece of paper with her name and
Phone number on it
I know you recognize her handwriting
But you tripped out and told me
She would never do that to me
Why are you lying C?
Don't worry about my business, take care of your own!
Bruh, how long have I known you?
Have I ever lied to you?
Maybe it wasn't my place to tell him or even prove it to him, but
Since he didn't believe me
I made it my business to show him that I was right
The invitation was there, and I took it
I was dead wrong for smashing his girl
But I felt he had to know
I couldn't let him go out like that
She gave me a pair of panties that he brought
If that wasn't proof enough
Was I that blind or just that stupid in defending him and myself?
I was trying to open his eyes
But what I did was destroy his trust in me and our friendship
Just because I was trying to prove a point

In My Past Life

In my past life
I must have been a womanizer or treated women very badly
Because I've suffered immensely in matters of the heart
In my attempts to make amends and make things right in this life
All the women of the world
Turned their backs on me simultaneously
Unaccepting of my attempts for appeasement
I yelled how much more do I need to learn and endure?
How much longer do I need to suffer?
How many times do I need to apologize?
All the women were discipline like female soldiers
Standing in formation like walls of stone statues
Waiting on some sort of command to speak
Not one head turned
No one moved
Volume and wisdom were spoken resoundingly loud
But no response was given
Silence was their answer as it echoed all around me
Like unseen chains to the eyes
I was kept bound to the accountability of my past life

No Love

I have two legs to stand on, but
How can I love another
When I can't even stand myself?

Learn to love and appreciate yourself because you won't have the ability to love and appreciate anyone else!

Blurred Lines

When we intermingle relationships
Blurred lines never come out with a clear concise picture
Just our growing baggage and irresponsibility
Drawn, speckled, and splattered
Then heavily brushed onto a weak canvas called dating
Our toxic and acidic behaviors seep into the fabric
Causing our emotions and hearts to give way like flooded ceilings
The pieces of our broken lives fall to the ground
Covering, soaking and staining what we desire most
True love

The Forecast

The forecast for the next few weeks
Definitely high tempers
The possibility of spontaneous and
Combustible conversations are very likely
The smell of charred hearts and
The feelings of scorched emotions fill the air
This presence, it's so familiar
Like De Ja Vu I've been here before
Many may be fooled by the deceptive smiles and
Sunny forecasts spoken by her lips
After intimacy
Yes, I'm okay
Yes, we are cool
I'm fine with just being your friend
But underneath I feel the turbulence of
Her cool outer shell giving way to every emotion boiling inside
It's been a few weeks since we last talked
Our forecast today, it's 75 degrees with sunny skies
But I also felt a cool and drafty wind blowing over my shoulder
In the distance, dark clouds form over the horizon
With an intensity I never felt before

Do not play with people's hearts, minds, and emotions! First impressions of trust and love can last a lifetime!

My Diagnosis

I felt like it was my duty as her friend with benefits
To help her in any way that I could
By no means am I a doctor or psychiatrist, but
My diagnosis, prognosis of her is that
She suffered from bad relationship fatigue,
Chronic depression, self-esteem issues and amnesia because
I could tell her a thousand times
How beautiful and smart she is
Reassure her that I needed her
Show her how relevant she is in my life
Make love to her as if it was our last day on earth
And before the night ended
It was if my actions meant nothing at all
Many days she would smile and blush at the sight of me
She would share the most beautiful things
Holding me near and within minutes
She could take that sweet moment
And have it take a turn for the worst
Like the human body with an aggressive cancer
I felt like it was my duty as her friend with benefits
To help her in any way that I could
By no means am I a doctor or psychiatrist,
But my diagnosis, prognosis of her is that
She suffered from bad relationship fatigue,
Chronic depression, self-esteem issues and amnesia because
If nurturing, complimenting and
Giving her those teachable moments were bottles of vintage wine
I served her in an ivory tuxedo
I poured those words into my best glasses and
Served them at room temperature
Sometimes chilled and she tossed them back at me
Like I just cursed her out undeservedly
Angry and out of sorts
I cleaned myself up the best way I could and
I walked away in a stoic silence
She rushed behind me grabbing my right arm begging me not to go
Her face was full of fear, anguish, and apology simultaneously
I could see her speaking and making gestures to make amends but

I was an unmanned vessel, separated by this vile moment yet again
This could have happened a hundred times since day one
Each outburst got worse and worse
Each day I remained with her
I drowned myself undeservingly in these deep and
Torrid waters of her diagnosis

Loving or being a friend to someone doesn't mean they have permission trample on you, hurt you or treat you any kind of way! Don't allow anyone to abuse or take advantage of your good heart, love and loyalty.

The Situation

Although she felt free from her situation
I know that my situation
Was causing her major complications
Got her emotions going back and forth
Round and round like clothes experiencing
Washer machine agitation
But from me to her
If it meant any consolation
I enjoyed her friendship and
Keeping it meant more to me than any part time relations
She told me she wanted to continue the situation but
I knew sooner or later someone is bound to get hurt and
Bring what we have to an end like segregation

Weigh your options wisely! If you plan to leave someone leave them first before entering a new friendship or relationship because someone is bound to get hurt!

The Situation II

The night she called me around 11:30 PM
Almost had me play racist with a female I was seeing
I would never ask a woman to come see me and
Have her drive forty plus minutes one way
Arriving, knocking, then calling for me to open the door and
I never answered, with two cars in my driveway
How could I explain this?
Unexpected company?
What ever happened to courtesy?
She could have called or texted me
To let me know that something had come up
My bladder must have stopped working
Because a brother was pissed
I wasn't letting this go
I was thankful I wasn't riding with my little friend
Like Clint Eastwood's movie, she was "Unforgiven!"
For seven consecutive days
She tried to contact me
Leaving messages saying she was sorry for falling asleep
That's bullshit, and talk is cheap
Her plan A or B showed up first and didn't want to leave
Or wanted to avoid confrontation
She wanted things to go back to the way they used to be
Before that night, but that wrong couldn't be made right
If I was a roach, her trust and name
Became like boric acid and bug spray
The righteousness man in me let her live and be free
Although she disagreed, hoping that one day, we will be
Removing myself from her proximity
Was the best thing for me and this situation

Guilty by Association

My actions and mannerisms were never really understood by others. People responded to me from the place they were in as opposed to relating to me as a individual. Like products from Dietz and Watson, I was presumed to be a dog because I ran the streets with a pack of dogs. I was the victim of stereotype, gender, and relationship profiling. I was guilty by association and sentenced before anything actually took place between us.

>*At the time I was dating*
>*I wasn't serious about anyone*
>*Nor was anyone serious about me*
>*It was sort of like entertainment, flipping channels on TV*
>*Trying to find a show that I really liked*
>*Days and nights of clicking the remote*
>*I finally found a channel that caught my attention*

I let my newest friend know that I needed a little time to get my house in order. I guess my house was built with a deck of cards because what happened in the next few weeks blew me away.

I thought my house was in pristine condition, but there were some stains I couldn't quite get out. I had no idea that a mutual acquaintance of ours was going behind my back telling my new friend how I was cleaning up my messes. I felt there was some uneasiness and mistrust toying with her mind but thank God she knew that I was clearing the path for us to be in a relationship. The second stain that remained came one night I was out with the pack. I wasn't hunting; I was being hunted. Hunted for reasons beyond my comprehension. I didn't know I was playing a game of chess. I didn't voluntarily sit down opposite of this woman's friend and move any pieces. She moved them in my absence. How convenient and unfair was that?

My new friend and her girlfriend had a falling out and weren't speaking. I didn't know I was the cause of their breach. I did what I could to help resolve the issue, but some things just can't be fixed with good intention.

Later that week I saw her girlfriend at the club
We talked about them getting back on speaking terms
And as the world turns
She wrote down her number and told me to call her
I thought we was on some we cool shit
I appreciate you looking out for me and my girl shit
But she was on some other shit
Some real cunning and disrespectful shit

I took the number without making an incident. In fact, I threw the number away, but I didn't think about how the situation could come back to haunt me. I should have called my new friend and let her know what happened, but I didn't. Our conversation had no implications of incrimination. I wasn't trying to holler at her. I was glad there was a possibility of them becoming friends again, just not on my account. I didn't think her girlfriend would use me as a way to get back into her good graces. A little birdie told me I was taking up too much of their time together. I was a threat coming between their friendship and I had to be stopped at any cost.

Unknowingly, I had become a stray dog seized by a phone call in the wee hours of the night. I was confined to my new friend's dog pound until trial. Seeing that my new friend had called me in my slumber I redialed the number but there was no answer. I got up, showered, got dressed to impress, feeling happy and blessed. I couldn't wait to go see her!

As I approached the walkway to her home
The door magically opened on its own
I wasn't greeted with the normal enthusiasm of a mega star
But there was much discontent
I didn't know I got suited up to come to my own trial
There was no set time or date
I guess it was on a need to know basis
I was served notice upon arrival, and she wasn't alone
Her mother, brother, his friend, her girlfriend, and another
Gentleman were in attendance
Did my reputation precede me?
I wasn't a bad person but according to whom
I was in the hot seat, surrounded by glares and stares

That would make anyone run to the nearest exit
Everyone there had his or her speech
I didn't get a chance to speak
I was interrupted every time I began to utter or
Show my teeth
Pardon the interruption, but
Why isn't her friend on trial here?
I finally realized this was a losing battle
No need for explanations or deliberations
I knew the final verdict
Like I was always told
Birds of a feather flock together
What makes me any different?
I took her friends number with no intent
I tossed the shit
But her friends' relevance and intent
It was all hearsay
It was entered as a confession and DNA evidence
It was all circumstantial
Made up and non-credible
But it was her testimony and allegiance that won them over
The jury was clearly biased
Did I take the number? Yes
Should I have put her in her place?
I felt there was no need to put her in her place
Did I call her? No
Did I hit on her? No
Could I have tried to holler at her behind my friends back? No
But their answers were yes!
Her girlfriend says, "He hangs out with trifling asses
So, he's a trifling ass!"
I wasn't about to be called too many more asses and
To keep the peace
I became in contempt of court and left
I was guilty by association or was it my character's assassination
I committed a kind act of stupidity and I paid dearly
Court is now adjourned
There's no need for an appeal
I'm guilty as charged in their hearts, minds, and eyes

Be careful of the company you keep! Your freedom, life, job and relationships may depend on it.

Conflicted

Conflicted, I hated to admit it
In secret, I wanted to erase the boundaries of our friendship
For something tangible and something real
Who wants to be living, surviving, and then dying
In a toxic relationship?
Not Me!
I just wanted to be me, love and live
Conflicted, I hated to admit it
We were great friends but
When I saw her walking with another guy at lunch
And she seemed to be having a good time, I was hurt
I was tow-up hurt
Like someone cracked a whip right across my heart
My heart ached like it never ached before
My stomach became nauseated
My face became twisted
Like I just bit into freshly sliced lemon halves but
I had no reason to feel jealous or be mad, but I was
It took everything I had to pull myself together
And get over what I was experiencing
I felt like turning around and walking the other way
But I stayed the course
I am glad she didn't see me
And even if she did
I wasn't ready to speak to her
I may have even ignored her
But I made up my mind that day
I would tell her how I really feel
I would not leave us to chance on this truly conflicting day

If you have feelings for someone don't be afraid to tell them. You will never know how they really feel or the outcome if you don't open your mouth or try!

Reasons of Uncertainty

As she peered into my eyes
I wondered what she saw in the mirrors of my soul
I could only image, but I hoped not to reveal anything too deep
Or the scars I had within
For it resembled the backs of my ancestors during the slave trade
Some of the wounds were still fresh and partially leaking
I didn't want to wipe the blood and pain of my past on someone
Else's garment of innocence
But I needed her, and she needed me
I needed her healing touch and
Her essence to tend and sooth my inner wounds
As I peered into her eyes
I could see concern, fear, and uncertainty of what may happen
After this one nightstand
She was certain I would end up hurting her
Leaving her alone to regret the day that she met me
But I made it hard for her to resist like giving alcohol or crack to a
Recovering addict free of cost and without judgement
I could see that this night would not be a typical touch and go
Although I was going to touch her and go
She could see that there was more to me than this
Six-two charismatic, gift of gab, flattery popping
I want you here and now persuasive toxin
She was posturing, verbally boxing but
My words were smooth like Jon B's, "Are You Down for Me?"
She calmed down and inhaled deeply like she just pulled on a blunt
I took her by the hand, and she held onto mine
Our imaginations and intentions took us to a beautiful place
Like Shirley Murdoch's, "As We Lay"
We went to a place where we could sooth each other's wounds
The next morning
Her reasons of uncertainty were as certain as life and death itself
I know she hoped to peer into my eyes again
I know she wanted to get to know me and
Become a permanent fixture in my life
But my lifestyle
I didn't have time for that
I didn't know whether I was going to live or die

Be free or be confined to jail, prison or be on the run
So, I vanished in the night with her only knowing my alias
And a fake number
Never peering into her eyes again

Pretending to offer something or care about someone to get what you want is wrong. The seeds you plant will come back to harvest one day! Get to know who you are dealing with on a platonic level before moving on to more serious circumstances! You will thank me later! One night of insignificant pleasure to one person may mean the world to another. When their world crashes yours will follow in turn.

360 Degrees

Several nights I laid awake wondering what happened?
What's going on?
Did we move too fast or was I too slow
Moving in the direction she wanted me to go?
Was it me?
What did I do?
I mean, I treated her right
The possibilities of a future between us seemed bright
Confused, the questions kept coming in my mind
Like a properly licked clitoris!
Twenty-one days seemed like a whole year
An eternity without her beside me
Her impression, her essence was embedded in me
Like damn, she is burning in me like data on CDs
Her personality, natural scent, hair, face, and curves
Played over and over again in my mind like automatic rewind
I was aware of everything around me, but I couldn't focus like
Broken photo lenses
I'm helplessly daydreaming
My hormones are feigning
Our emotional and spiritual connection was broken
Almost pushed me to the brink of extinction
No contact no show
Had me feeling like a crushing blow to the male genitals
It started in my heart and cursed every part of my body
I was feverish, I was sick
I couldn't eat
I couldn't sleep
And for the first time I experienced being heartbroken
I was vulnerable, and the shoe was on the other foot
For three months
I lay deep in its belly
Slowly being devoured by the hurt and
Pain that I've caused so many in my past

Ghosting or disappearing from someone's life, no matter the reason, is selfish, immature, and very hurtful. It can be potentially dangerous for either person. It's all fun and games until the shoe is on the other foot!

Sincerely Yours (The Boomerang Affect)

When I gave her my number
I should have gotten hers that same night
She said that she worked as a registered nurse and that
She never had any real free time
After a few weeks went by I almost forgot about her
I was completely caught off guard
When she called early one Saturday morning
She asked was I free for the afternoon and evening
I said yes
She said that it would her treat
We hung out and got to know each another a little better
She wined and dined me
She bought me a bottle of my favorite libation
We stopped by a local store and
She surprised me by taking me to the condom section
She purchased those too
She even paid for the hotel room
After a great evening
I awoke alone with a note that stated
Thank you for an amazing day
Sorry I couldn't be there when you awoke
I'm in a complicated relationship
The first time I saw you I had to have you
I'd appreciate it if you try not to contact or find me
I'll contact you
You were truly wonderful
Sincerely yours
With red lipstick imprinted in the form of a kiss
Underneath the salutation

The Corridor of Contemplation

Standing wet in the corridor of contemplation
My umbrella was useless in the gusty winds and
Torrential rains at home
My heart, mind and emotions were my feet and counterweight
They became unbalanced as I began to slip
Then slide further down the corridor of contemplation
Another's sunshine, blue skies and warm weather greeted me
At the other end of the corridor with open arms
Ready to receive me
I spent weeks in the corridor of contemplation
As the storms at home
Raged on day after day and night after night
I was wet, weak, and cold
My loins were hot and full of desire
I was ready to fire and
It was getting harder and harder to hold my footing
As the wind and pelting rain eroded the moral grounds beneath me
The angle of the corridor was now at a full 180 degrees
Temptation pulled on every resisting muscle
And thought in my body
Then gravity overtook me
I stopped fighting and let go
Falling into the clear skies, warmth, and comfort
That I sought at home

In the Dark

In the Dark
I was her everything
I was her coffee in the morning
Her sunshine on rainy days
I was her breath of fresh morning air
I was the rhythm to her heartbeat
I was the man in her dreams waking her up wet
I was the friend who gave her the confidence to believe in herself
And fight during her darkest hours of depression
I was her inspiration to write a happy chapter
In a book well deserved closed, but
When you become so special and mean so much to one person
It can become too much to bare
Especially if that person belongs to someone else
What we shared was everything she should have gotten at home
But she was neglected
She began seeking what she was missing
What she found was warm and clear like Bermuda's water
She swam deep in my waters and never wished to come up for air
In the dark, we went well together like cookies and milk
We were close like ass on seats, skulls, and sutures
We were tight like twenty-twos on Escalades, Yukons, or Denalis
I was her key to absolute freedom
And she could fly free for a period of time
Unrestricted mentally, verbally, and physically
We touched intimately but we couldn't bond spiritually
Sparking something that felt totally right
But consciously and morally it was wrong
She did things to me that felt right, it was natural
Where at home it was a chore
She felt like a whore or a trick
Prostituting for financial security, a white picket fence
A dog, a Mercedes, the Joneses
I couldn't imagine being in a place where
Communication was like embracing a cactus
Where love was an endangered species and

Was about to become extinct
She was a withering flower in a barren desert
And rain wasn't soon to come
She was torn between two worlds and a fence
For her, the grass was greener on the other side,
But she was bound by obligation, a piece of paper and
A promise that was not meant to be broken

In the dark
Things went flawlessly well for nearly half a year
We avoided any potential storms together
And without warning a series of fifty-foot, rogue waves
Decimated this warm and tranquil oasis
The rules we had in place to sustain what we had
Begun to fade like ink on old receipts
Some part of me believed that she wanted him to know
Deep down she wanted him to hurt and suffer like she had
Who wants to be neglected, lied to, taken for granted
And cheated on for years
His behavior had created a sassy, cut your eyes, size six waist
Bouncing with attitude to a mean groove
Like James Brown's, "The Big Pay Back" in five-inch heels
She danced all day and all night to a rebellious tune
And blindly broke our curfew agreement
And every other agreement
Because she no longer wanted to go home at night
I began losing respect for her when
She no longer gave any priority to her obligations
At home or her children
I didn't want to see her get hurt
Nor cut off her nose in spite her face
I could care less about him
Maybe it was blind love
Maybe it was revenge
Maybe she really wanted to make him suspicious, jealous, or mad
Maybe she really didn't care anymore and was ready to move on
Maybe she wanted to prove to him that she could get a man
At her age with two children
Maybe it was all of the above
These were significant questions that were about to be answered

In the dark she used to say
I'm so tired of not being able to be seen with you
I'm so tired of hiding the feelings that I have for you
I can't sleep at night because I want to be next to you
In the dark we're so special, so special

I don't know what happened between them
Or what he said to her but
Everything she agreed not to do in the beginning
Happened explosively like the eruption of Krakatoa
Her style of dress and hair went from a conservative and cute mom
To an executive of sexiness and style overnight
I wasn't one to complain but
I had problems keeping my eyes in my head
Let alone picking my lower jaw up off the floor
To see a woman leave home like that and you are on bad terms
With her, creates war and torment of the mind, heart and soul

I never really wanted her to meet my kids or family
Unless we were in a serious relationship but that changed
When she began to show up unannounced at my home and
Places I went to frequently
She began calling and texting me from her cell phone
Which was jointly owned with her other half
She bought me gifts with a credit card they both used and
She didn't care who knew or who saw us together anymore
It blew my friends and coworkers away
That we were seeing each other for nearly a year
And no one knew about it
Maybe she was really planning to move on
Or was there something else at work here?

What happens in the dark eventually comes to the light
Even if you wanted it to stay there
Intrigued by her latest and brash actions
Her husband clearly took notice this time
Like falling stars lighting up the night sky
Like any man subject to vulnerability in his relationship
He was beyond hurt and wanted her back

He suddenly remembered the value of his vows and his family
He suddenly remembered how important she was in his life
He suddenly remembered the woman he fell in love with years ago
He suddenly remembered the woman he had conveniently forgotten for someone else
He suddenly got that ill feeling of another man
Making his woman smile in ways he should have for years
He suddenly had a fear of losing his wife to man much younger
More handsome, fitter, and treated her like a queen
Not a game, a book, or a possession
Placed on a shelf until he felt like being bothered

In the dark
I had no idea that we were already in the light
A California brush fire, hundreds of miles wide
Bright enough to be seen from space
I'm guilty of writing chapters in her husband's book
Chapters he wishes he had written, but failed to write
Chapters he wanted to erase and rewrite quickly without me in it
I had no knowledge that he knew about me
Information that was given to him at their counseling sessions
Confessed by hers truly
She promised me that this would never happen
I couldn't believe she gave up my government and where I worked
She might as well have given them
My home address and blood type
I began receiving threatening letters from him at the job, and
Pressure from my Superiors to cease and desist communication and
Contact with her or lose my employment
I felt betrayed and used like
Edmond Dantes in "The Count of Monte Cristo"
I kept asking myself, how could she?
If I was ever asked about our relationship
I would have downplayed our involvement together, but
It's too late for that
If she needed to confess
She should have gone to a Catholic Church or God himself
The situation would have stayed between me, her,
The man in the booth or God
Finite

In the dark
What she used to say no longer mattered to me anymore
She couldn't have been that tired of not being able to see me
Or hiding how she truly felt with her actions and behaviors
As much as I enjoyed the song sung by Keith Sweat
I knew what we had would not *Last Forever*
The time was fast approaching, and we would have to part ways
Presumably, like grown folk, but
I can see and agree if it got out of hand
The more I thought about it
There was a fine line between a situationship and
Becoming a pawn in a lover's quarrel
In the midst of it all I became the pawn
Something I didn't expect or appreciate, but I had to accept it
When she confessed at counseling
I knew she was still in love with her husband
I knew she wanted that feeling of security and her family back
I wasn't ready to take on the sacrifice
Of merging another family with my own
After my divorce, my three kids were enough
I wouldn't sacrifice their well-being and
Lifestyle for something I wanted and
It may not have worked out long term

The fight that ensued for her really didn't exist
I could have easily persuaded her to be with me anytime I chose
She truly wished to postpone and stagger the separation over time
But I didn't have the time or energy for it
Too much had happened for me to indulge or trust her again
I wasn't going to compete for something I knew I already had
There was no point in winning
Winning would have resulted in the loss of a life
And freedom for a man, in addition to the separation of family units
Needing healing from adults making
Bad decisions that once felt like the right thing to do
I did what was best for us all
I let her go

I wished them well, and it's something that he couldn't understand
But one thing is for certain
He will never neglect or treat her like she doesn't matter
Or exist ever again!

The morals to the story are that another man's trash is another man's treasure! Any relationship that is built without integrity will fall without integrity! Relationships based on dependency exist, but it rarely feels like your forever after!

Consumed with Worry

When we dated
She was too worried about what my position and job title was
She was too worried about finding a knight in shining armor
To fix her financial woes
She was too worried about the type of automobile I was driving
Although she didn't have one of her own
She was too worried about where she was being taken for
Breakfast, lunch, and dinner, but it was never her treat
She was too worried about what people were saying about us
At work
She was too worried about who was calling or texting me
Outside of herself
She was too worried about who my friends were and
Where we hung out
She was too worried about hiding her past
To receive love in the future
She was too worried about failed relationships that
She never truly got over
She was too worried to realize she had a good thing
She was too worried about her insecurities to let me in
She was too worried about herself to be concerned with me
She was caught up in being too worried and
Wondered why I walked away

Informed Decision

It was rare for a woman to ask a man out
She had been asking me for months
I wasn't putting up a front but intuitively I felt reservation
There was a hesitation in my gut, and I didn't know why
But I gave into desire's eye
I was single and *lawd* she was fine
There, I digress, I finally said yes
Excited, she was at a loss of words and as the world turns
I didn't want to call her a liar
But because she wasn't forthcoming about
Who he really was to her in their relationship
And what was going on after their separation
She took away my ability and choice to make an informed decision
A safer decision if I still chose to meet with her
She invited me to her place for dinner and a movie
The man she called her X was still officially her husband and
Although they were separated, he still had a key to her apartment
She gave him false hope and inspiration
By having sex with him a few days prior to our date
It was a decision that almost cost us our lives
He showed up that night unannounced to discuss reconciliation,
But he was greeted with the realization that she was moving on
With her life
Because his dream was shattered
He felt that he needed to end ours waving a gun
No one got hurt that night but
We could have easily been killed, maimed, crippled or
Placed on life support
I know she didn't mean for any of this to happen
But because it happened, she will no longer have the opportunity
To be forthcoming in my life ever again

Selfish

When I said that she was selfish
I wasn't given a chance to finish my sentence
I was immediately cut off
Like NY City drivers forcing their way into merging lanes,
Horns blaring and traffic is at a stand still
So selfish, Bush Administration-ish
She heard only what she wanted to hear
Then declared war based on premeditated experiences,
Beliefs and accusations
When I said that she was selfish
I never said that she didn't give
But what she gave wasn't free
Nor was it given from the heart
Those she helped heard about her gifting
Like the latest songs repeated in radio rotation
She kept detailed mental notes
Tabs for her own brand of recoupment
Her selflessness came with a price
Much greater than any good deed plus interest
It's a price I will never ask for or pay her ass ever again!

If you truly give from your heart do not expect anything in return!

Did She Consider

No matter how many times she asked me
What did I wanted to eat?
Did I like this sweater?
Did I like those jeans?
Did I like those shoes?
Did I want to see a specific movie?
Did I like that car?
And I gave my honest opinion
Why is she still asking me am I sure?
Try it on
It looks very nice
It tastes good
Test drive the car

I'm confused,
I must not know what I like or what my own tastes are
What about how I like to dress?
What about the foods I like to eat?
Did she ever consider that?
Was she buying clothes for me or for herself?
Did my opinion ever really matter?

There is nothing wrong with supporting someone else's taste in you, but when your own taste and likes don't matter in a relationship, it's not a relationship, it's a Dictatorship!

The Perfectly Placed Call*

The perfectly placed call is what said it all
Because she had no reason to withhold information or lie to me
When we opened up to one another
And shared our past and present experiences
The basis we agreed upon to solidify this relationship
Was on open communication, honesty, and truth
I didn't want to play another game of Clue
Who done who, what, when where and why?
I was tired of pulling out the magnifying glass
Putting on a trench coat, revisiting facts, lies and half truths
Like a black Sherlock Holmes, the Super Sleuth
I remember her words as if we had this conversation yesterday
I remember the sincerity in her eyes, face, and voice
Stating that her ex is no longer in the picture and
That she didn't communicate with him anymore
Except by her work phone only to finalize their divorce details
She even went as far as getting a new cell phone number
Stating that this is a number that he didn't have
Who was she trying to convince; him, me, or herself?
I didn't care that she talked to him because
I'm not jealous or naive
That was her statement and choice
I just held her to it
I have an ex-wife and female friends that I'm cool with
They know their boundaries
I know my boundaries
I trusted that she knew hers and would do the same
But the perfectly placed call is what said it all
Because she had no reason to withhold information or lie to me

     After spending a tumultuous weekend with her out of town I had many questions about where we stood and whether I should continue the relationship. On our way back to Virginia, I was still fuming about several incidents that took place over the weekend. At the time, I didn't have much to talk about. Two hours into the drive her cell phone rings and a familiar name from the past had come up on the screen ID. I grabbed the phone and turned it over before she could see who was calling and I said, "Your phone is ringing are you going to answer it?"

She said, "No, I'll call the person back later, I'm driving!"

I replied, "Answer it or I'll answer it for you!"

She didn't answer and continued to drive.

I said, "I'll call him back!"

She sat scared and motionless searching for something to say, but no words came out. I couldn't escape the painful situation that sunk it's fangs into me. As the venom set in, I wasn't able to control the escalating thoughts and emotions coursing through my veins. I threw the phone at her not knowing where it hit or fell but it left my hand with velocity and harmful intent. I needed to get out of the car quickly and get as far away from her as possible or I was most certainly going to choke her. I would have used hydraulic like pressure, squeezing with both hands until they were filled with a pile of mush and skin. I felt stupid and betrayed but mostly hurt. With every second that passed by, my anger grew to the equivalent of a thousand Hulks, but I remained calm as possible not to kill the both of us while she was driving.

When a person isn't forthcoming, I clearly saw how hurtful and detrimental that it can be to the trust and survival of a relationship. I was usually the bigger person when it came to talking about our issues peacefully, but this time was different. I went right into it like a high school coach ripping his team, losing big at halftime. Decibels, I'm sure the aliens heard me in deep space yelling, "Why didn't you tell me that you gave him the cell phone number? How long have you been talking to him behind my back? Were you ever going to tell me? We talk every day, so the opportunity was there. I shouldn't have had to find out like this! A fucking phone call and not from the horse's mouth!"

She said, "I didn't mean for this to happen and I'm sorry. You're right, I should've told you!"

In a mocking voice I said, "It's a little too late for that shit, but you still want me to accept your apologies, forgive, love and trust you unconditionally."

Then I asked, "What else have you done that you haven't told me about since we're on the subject?"

All this could have been prevented if she were honest and truthful, not being a mockery of its meaning and what she portrayed to be. The distance she placed between us could never be made whole knowing her mindset, who she is and what she's capable of doing. I thank God for the perfectly placed call because I may have never known the truth behind the secrets she was keeping.

Mistaken Identity

For months, I didn't know what was wrong with me, at least that's what I said. I felt frustrated, tired, and drained. I had this constant feeling of running uphill or moving against the grain in this relationship. I was facing immense obstacles like salmon swimming upstream to their spawning grounds.

I was worn out
Trying to make things work in the relationship
Or was I the only one trying?
I had hope and hope had me feeling like
One last try may bring sunshine for all time

In one last effort, I traveled out of town with my ex-girlfriend's girlfriend to visit her for a few days. Prior to that, we were on the ropes for months. I prayed for God to open my eyes and show me what I needed to see to break free. The answer came almost immediately in the form of mistaken identity. Identification that cannot be explained to me as being a mistake.

For brunch at her favorite restaurant in front of a mutual friend, the cashier asks my girlfriend at the time, "Where is your Spanish speaking husband?"

Confused I said, "Are you talking to her or are you talking about me?"

The cashier said, "No, not you, her husband!"

There was no mistaken identity. There was confidence and conviction in her eyes and voice. She didn't stutter or stammer. She was absolutely sure! My girlfriend at the time claimed that she didn't know what the cashier was talking about. I definitely don't speak Spanish fluently or speak it publicly. I didn't live in the same state as her. This is her favorite restaurant, she loves to eat, and if it wasn't me who was it? There was nothing she could say to explain it away. There was no rug to sweep it under. There were too many small coincidences that added up to one huge conclusion. She had been lying and cheating the whole time we were together. There's no more makeup gifts or makeup sex to smooth over or cover up the lies. There is no more minimizing the obvious. What I told her next was no mistake. Identify this, we are done!

We have a natural defense system against liars and cheaters. It's called intuition, aka that gut feeling. Listen to it and trust it, not the mouths of human beings that don't have you best interest in mind!

Isolated

Two and a half years of wrestling with denial
The truth finally slammed me on my back and
All the fight and air had forcefully been removed from my body
As I tried to get back up
Realization's power gave me a two-piece
I got a chin check of pristine clarity and a left hook to the body
I seized up and fell back to the ground cringing in pain
My mouth was wide open gasping for air
Every situation that I endured with her
Flashed before me like it was my last breath
Each memory was the brick and
Mortar that built this fortress of isolation around me
It was designed with no doors or visible windows
Just her and I inside
Holding my head in my hands
I asked myself how did I allow this to happen?

Isolated,
I was being detained, quarantined and
Tested for new weakness
Not for the healing or the growth of our relationship
It was for the progression of separation from the world that
I knew and loved so much

Isolated,
I was the one thing that she couldn't share with anyone else
Not with my children, mother, family, friends,
Dreams, or aspirations
I was slowly being separated from them all like oil and water
Like pieces of a broken figurine that tape or
Glue couldn't hold together

Isolated,
I became a prisoner of her crafty words and behaviors
I was coerced into not having any relationships or
Dealings outside of our own
I was put under constant fear
That she would try to harm or kill herself

In her eyes, whenever I wasn't acting right
She would threaten to cut up or
Burn my personal things when I wasn't at home
As a last resort, knowing I had issues with the law
Whenever I said I was leaving her or didn't do what she asked
She would threaten to call the police and turn me in

Isolated,
My family and friend's names
Were flogged with accusations
She tried to turn me against them and them against me
She accused anyone of the opposite sex
Of cheating or they want to be with me
These rants could go on for hours and
Seemed like days in this maze of insanity

Isolated,
She had my mind and emotions tied up
Fighting the ghosts of her insecurities at every waking moment
Going to the bathroom or walking into another room
Outside of her eyes view, triggered quick feet
Her ears up like a German Shephard
Listening, waiting, and anticipating
Trying to control my every move
Impeding my thoughts of lucidity, reasoning
And escaping to freedom
The power and control I gave her
Dissipated like dew drops in the morning Sun
The horns had sounded and like the Walls of Jericho
The fortress that had been built around me came tumbling down
As the dust settled, I climbed atop the rubble triumphant
In a war she thought I couldn't win being isolated

Don't allow anyone to poison your mind and push you away from your family, and friends Lesson two, don't allow a relationship to stop you from doing the things you enjoy doing most.

Violated

We were living together prior to our breakup
We were clearly not together but we temporarily shared a place
No matter what she had done to me
No matter what we been through together
I never called any unfamiliar names or numbers in her cell phone
I never went through her phone reading text messages
I never tried to access her email looking for information
I never went through her pants, jeans or
Purses looking for numbers
I never ransacked her drawers looking at her paperwork, receipts,
Bank statements or personal mail
I never tried to break the password on her cell phone, laptop
Or computer
But maybe I should have because I truly felt violated
The day she became the intruder
Encroaching on everything that was personally my own
Like acid reflux,
I done everything in my power to make her heartburn, but
She had no right to go through my personal things
Without my permission
Her excuse was that she believed I was leaving her
For another woman
Acting like she wasn't a co-conspirator in our demise, but
A victim in a relationship crime she had no part of
She didn't want to look at the woman in the mirror and
Conveniently dismissed the crazy mood swings,
False accusations, lies, bizarre, selfish, and single like behaviors
But out of the blue, I purposely broke her heart and ruined her life

Violated,
If there were any grounds for reconciliation or
Revisiting any possibilities of a friendship in the future
Are now gone
My restraint was purposely hidden like condoms and
You and your significant other don't use them anymore
I stood stoic in disbelief
That she had gone through my personal things
Searching for that ah ha moment

Deflecting and trying to shift the blame
When we weren't together anymore
I didn't have anything to hide
So why question me like Socrates?
She better step back
She doesn't want to box me
Baby girl is about to get checked like hockey
I was beyond angry, and I began to see red
My mind and soul were going to a dark place without any light
I knew if I got to her
Before she ran and barricaded herself in the bedroom
The expression of burying someone in their own back yard
Could have become reality

Violated,
I calmed down enough to gather myself and think
I grabbed my cell phone and
Headed out the front door to my car
I needed a lifeline like "Who Wants to Be a Millionaire" because
I had a million thoughts and
A million feelings that could have got me
A Million years and front-page coverage in the daily news

Have you ever been violated when you have done your best to be a good person and stay monogamous in a relationship detrimental to your health and well-being? For your own good get out of this situation quickly and don't look back!

Euthanized

She euthanized me by day
Reanimated me by night
Bringing me forth from emotional and physical coffin
She illuminated the worst in me and
In return, she received the worst in me
I no longer knew what love or happiness felt like
Our commonality was our physical needs
A place where we temporarily agreed
Only because we were familiar with one another
Each day I internally grieved
There was no bereavement in becoming a matrimonial zombie
Waking and participating, but dying deeper on the inside every day
I had no more energy to be reanimated
Or carry out this charade
So, I refused to breathe
Not filling my lungs or heart with false hope
Knowing I was returning to a relationship clearly underwater
Never to see the light of day ever again

This Is Not Love

Our desire to have a committed relationship is not in question
Our like and attraction for one another is strong like nature itself
Our emotions run deep like the depths of the ocean
Moving and flowing as the waves of thoughtless incidents
Come surfacing, crashing, and cutting mercilessly into our minds
And hearts like rock, sand, and limestone
Our interactions with one another turn the sea red daily
But rarely reach the eyes of those on the surface
The world sees the show, the circus
Not the lion and lioness jostling for the title of trainer
Fighting for control, power, and dominance
In a place where it is not meant to be
We are in a union but far from being together
There is no trust, peace, or reprieve
We are immersed in blankets of tension
Our bedding and mattress don't feel comfortable anymore
I can describe many things this relationship is
But I know what we have is not love

The Wrong Person

It's funny how the wrong person
Keeps showing you that they are the wrong person in your life
They will do anything except the right thing
Like leaving you alone or just walking away after a breakup
She would rather dial my work and cell phone number fifty times
Back-to-back like it was a family emergency
She would rather sit outside my apartment like
She was going to get an invitation to come in
Refusing to leave the hallway or parking lot
Like her name was on the lease
She would rather annoy me using online software to spy on me
Trying to see who was calling, texting, or emailing me
News flash, we are not together anymore!
How was any of her actions
Going to change the way I felt about her in a positive way?
She didn't care if her actions were harmful to me, herself or
Anyone else
To prevent any further actions to undermine our boundaries
I filed a restraining order against her before I committed an act
Where I would be pursued by the Fraternal Order
She was notified not to come around or
Contact me for any reason
She went way past that fine line between harassment
And a felony crime
I thank God I didn't act out of total anger and frustration
Because I was the right one
To behave like the *wrong person!*

Break ups can be very hurtful and intense! Stalking or harassing someone won't bring the relationship back! It's not worth It! Leave the person alone! It is easy to get into trouble and hard to get out of it! Would you want someone stalking or harassing you or worse?

Romance

The romance in me was something that I lost
Traveling the roads of would be loves
And intimate friends supposed to be's
My romance became tired
Invisible, ruffed up, tattered remnants of so-called relationships
Scattered throughout skeleton closet burial grounds

Buying flowers, holding hands, taking walks in the park, picnics
Sharing our dreams gazing into the night sky, blind fold fun
Rose petals leading to the bed, cuddling, massages
Lit candles, aromatherapy, hot baths, and
Taking showers together
Are all characteristics of romance
Once I,
Were abused and unappreciated by women
So, I resented and eliminated it
Slowly relearning to open my heart
Ever preparing,
Savoring and growing romance as a fruit
Only feeding that special someone
Who deserves to taste its sweetness
Romance

I'm So Tired

I'm so tired of arguing
I'm so tired of fighting
I'm so tired of being frustrated dealing with her
I'm so tired of making excuses for the way she acts
I'm so tired of hearing her say I'm sorry
I'm so tired of makeup sex and make up gifts
When they truly don't have any value or meaning
Especially when the issues I keep talking about
Are getting worse and she hasn't attempted to fix any of them
Damn, wouldn't you be tired too?

I Didn't Leave Because of You

I didn't leave the relationship because of you
I left the relationship for me
To regain my peace of mind and spirit
To restore everything, I lost in you
Taking the time out to find myself and enjoy my life once again

Don't get so deep in a relationship that you lose yourself in the process of supporting and loving someone else! It may be easy to get into a relationship, but it is a million times harder to get out once you lose yourself in it.

Black and White

For a longtime
The decisions and interactions I made with people
Were in black and white
It was either yes or no
You do or you don't
I had no time for maybes
I didn't leave any room for gray area because
When you give people more options
To play with your time and heart
They will do just that

When a Woman Cares

When a woman cares about a man
She will have his back and support him like no other
When a woman loves a man
She will put him first over many things in her life
Even her family or children
But like a car in a terrible wreck, don't get it twisted
Don't take what she is giving you for granted
When she is getting tired, and she no longer cares
When that Godlike treatment stops
Know that you have done something terribly wrong!
Know that your time with her is going to be short
If you can fix it
Fix it, and do her right
If not, walk away gracefully
Or she will mummify you alive like the Egyptian Priest, but
There's no afterlife in the relationship
The chances of maintaining or
Rebuilding that fondness, trust, and openness
That you had in the beginning
Are like winning the lottery and you lost the ticket
When a woman doesn't care anymore

When you have someone special in your life treat them right the first time! There may not be a second chance to prove your worth or get them back!

Looking Out

My good friend and I were roommates for over a year. We are both positive brothers so when he approached me about his younger brother needing a place to live upon being released from prison, I was eager to help, but my intuition said no. I overrode my instincts because I know what I've been through in my life. I was given help and being able to mentor and give another brother an opportunity at a fresh start meant a lot. It was a way to look out and help was being asked for by a good person.

I had a chance to talk to my friend's younger brother to see where his heart and mind was at. I was not sure if I would have taken the chance if I hadn't talked to my friend's brother first. At the time, his heart and mind seemed to be in the right place, so I agreed to move forward. This was based on the condition that he would do as he proclaimed. That was to be respectful of my kids, household, clean up behind himself and find work. As a condition of his release, he wasn't supposed to go back to his old neighborhood, use or sell drugs or violate other rules of his probation. After his release from prison, we had celebrated and made plans to take him job hunting. Who gets a job his first week out of prison? A pretty good job with health benefits working for the state. I applied several times with the state and had no luck. With all the positive conversations and reinforcements, things seemed to be taking an optimistic turn in his life. Everyone makes mistakes but life is about how you bounce back from those mistakes and do better. He was provided all meals and given bus money to get back and forth to work until he received his first check. How blessed can a man be in this position? I never expected the red apple to turn brown so quickly.

The third week after his release a police officer and a detective stopped by the apartment on my day off. They were inquiring the whereabouts of my friend's brother. I placed myself in jeopardy by telling them what I thought was the truth, but it turned out to be a lie. I advised the police officer and detective that he was at work and would be in later that evening. I had to use all my wits to talk them out of staying at my apartment until he arrived. I wasn't a hundred percent sure my friend's brother was at work. I didn't want them going up there to look for him and risk his employment. He had just got the job. I didn't want him to violate his probation either. I took their card and told them that he would contact them as soon as he got in. I was told he was involved in an incident in his old neighborhood. A place he wasn't supposed to be. If his probation officer were aware of this, he would be in violation of his probation and headed back to jail. I called my friend and advised him of the situation in case he happened to see or contact his brother first. I got this eerie feeling that he hadn't been at work or got fired. I called his job and the supervisor confirmed my fear. He had missed two days his first week and a no call no show twice this week. I begged for his job to be reinstated but it was too late. The damage had been done. I was told that his mouth and negative attitude didn't help his chances either. I couldn't believe what I was hearing and what was happening. The get out prison speech was just a speech. I was deeply disappointed. I felt used for doing a good thing. Sometimes when you look out for someone, they are looking out for themselves and do not care about the consequences or how their actions affect other people and their own lives. When he came back to the house his brother and I both confronted him about the situation. Even after being told the truth, he didn't get it. He was trying to evade and deflect the situation. He was attempting to make it seem like everyone else was lying and getting on him for no good reason. He made excuse after excuse like we were the ones who had gotten him fired and how we weren't really looking out for him. His brother and I both got tired of talking to him and said, "If you can't get it together you know where you headed back to!"

I gave him the card the detective left for him.

He said, "I will call them in the morning!"

He claimed had no idea why they were looking for him. I felt he knew what was going on all along. I also knew he wasn't going to call them, but he was informed. The following Thursday, his probation officer left her card with my neighbor downstairs because no one was home when she stopped by to visit. I called her to see what was going on. He hadn't checked in, called or been to any of his appointments in a few weeks. The gavel was about to come down on him once again. He was a decision and a signature away from going back to prison. The effort was there, but we couldn't save him from himself.

The next day around 5 p.m., I went to pick up my kids for the weekend and I dropped them off at the apartment. I ran to the store to pick up a few things and grab some pizza for dinner. I hadn't been gone fifteen minutes when I got a call from my kids saying there's a man and woman downstairs banging on the front door and ringing all the doorbells. They were shouting for my friend's brother. They wouldn't stop banging on the door or leave. Scared to death for their safety, I left the grocery cart in the middle of the aisle. I raced home, tires screeching in the middle of the street. I jumped out of my car with bad intentions. I grabbed a crowbar from my trunk and started yelling at the trespassers on my porch. As I ran up the walkway, they turned their attention to me and climbed over to another porch and started running down the street. I gave chase for a block or two and told them never to come back here again. I didn't know if they were robbers, crack heads, had guns or what. As long as my children were safe, I was fine. I didn't know if he sold them drugs in the house or on the porch, but I was pissed they showed up at my residence under those circumstances. When someone scares the hell out of me and puts my kids in danger over something that he did, there was no more looking out! I'm blessed it went well because it could have ended much worse. When I advised his brother of what happened I was asked to give him another chance. That chance came and went when he lied about working and his whereabouts for weeks. That chance died when he sold drugs in or near my house and put my kids in danger. That chance was buried when I received multiple visits from a cop, a detective, a probation officer, and a pair of crackheads at my door all in a months' time. I didn't have this much traffic or drama in my home, and I was single, singing "D". How many times do you have to explain something to a grown man? He is very intelligent. He has to go!

My friend says, "If you put him out you put me out too!"

I replied, "Brother, think about it, but it's your choice. This didn't have to happen, but your brother chose this without any regard for those around him; just like I did many years ago at my parent's home. There is no respect, accountability, or appreciation for what had been done for him. He has been deceitful and bullshitting us from the beginning. I didn't have to agree to any of this and I will not enable him to continue his behavior here, bro! "

I felt really bad I had to let both of them go. After their mother died, they only had each other. Brothers' looking out for each other no matter what, but to a fault. I admire that. I wished them both well and I hope there wouldn't be any hard feelings, but I couldn't continue to look out for someone who didn't care about those who were truly looking out for him, especially under those circumstances.

Looking Out II

I didn't really know this man. I saw him a few times at my grandmother's church. He was always personable and dressed nicely. I assumed he was a good person. I was walking downtown Market Street toward the Wilmington Library and ran into this gentleman on a hot, summer day. We talked for a few minutes and he asked me did I know of any companies that were hiring. Looking out, I advised him to apply at the company I was working for and told him to use me as a reference. The following week I saw him in company uniform. He thanked me for helping him get the job. He mentioned that the interview panel spoke very highly of me. As we were about to depart, he asked to borrow twenty dollars for lunch until he got paid. I didn't really have it to give, but looking out, I allowed him to borrow the twenty dollars. It has always been hard for me to see another person go hungry or do without. Two weeks went by rather quickly. I wasn't pressed about the twenty dollars I was owed. I wanted to see how he was doing, if he liked the job, and how the company was treating him. As I was headed towards the main office, the sun was shining brightly and out of nowhere, torrential rain fell from the skies without warning. In the pouring rain, I spotted him walking downtown in regular street clothes.

I asked, "Are you off today?"

He said, "No, they let me go!"

I said, "What happened?"

They said, "I stole a woman's purse. I didn't steal it. I saw it and returned it to the office where I found it."

It was very unfortunate because I recommended him for the job. He was also in company uniform representing himself, all minorities, and the employer at the same time. Totally drenched, my mood matched the gloomy weather outside. I was consumed with resentment, anger, and disappointment. I reached the main office dripping wet. I asked to speak to the man as if I didn't know what happened to him. I was told their rendition of the story and my mouth dropped in total shock.

Before I began to say anything my boss and the owner says," Don't worry it wasn't your fault. It doesn't affect you or the way we feel about you in any way. No one knew he would steal a client's purse, take the contents, and then claim to be a hero by bringing it back after he emptied it. It was all on video surveillance tape."

No matter how I tried to get over it or dismiss it, deep down inside I was affected. I felt the situation did change the way the company perceived and felt about me as an employee. How could it not? I felt as though my name, credibility, and character were tainted and assassinated by this man for trying to look out!

When a person, company or organization looks out for you appreciate what has been done for you! Don't pay them back with regret and disappointment!

Fun Dummy

My fun dummy days led me to a place
Where I compromised my choice to continue this path freely
Confined by the law
My lifestyle went from a drag racing to a crawl
Hanging with my peoples, Ms. Party and Mr. Alcohol

Living in the fast lane and having too much fun without moderation will cause you major problems sooner or later! Slow down!

The Breaking Point

There were several times in my life
Where I reached my breaking point
No matter how much love and good I had to share
It was never enough
I was never accepted
Like receiving news from a doctor that I had an incurable disease
I lived in a world where selfishness, ego, pride, greed,
Manipulation, anger, hate, and despair was an invasive species
With no natural known predators
It took over where love, togetherness, communication,
Compromise, and community once thrived
Acts of selflessness, caring, and goodness were treated negatively
Like I was a leper or unwanted child
In this world, I couldn't be myself and it seemed I didn't fit in
No matter what I done to enhance my life and
Do for others I was fed shit in return
For all my efforts there was no prize or consolation to be won
I did not see the lessons in this if there were any to be learned
There was nothing to look forward to
And I reached my breaking point
For many years I woke up living in a bad dream of mental and
Emotional torment
If I went to sleep experiencing nightmares and woke up to
Experience the same
I wished not to be in either, so I chose

If you are having erratic thoughts, feelings of helplessness, depression or suicidal thoughts, reach out and ask for help! Be responsible and accountable for your own wellbeing! No one may understand or recognize that you need help until it is too late! Don't wait!

Hopeless and Broken

Before my descent into darkness
I was beyond tired mentally, emotionally, physically,
And spiritually
Debris at the bottom of the deepest ocean
Are the best words I could find to describe the weight I felt
Imagine I was that pebble or stone
Skipping over the dark, murky, brown water, unable to stay afloat
Looking upward, I began sinking with no resistance
Bubbles from my nose and mouth ascended to the surface
No one saw or heard my cries for help and
Just as the ripples started at the surface
They faded away as if the water was never disturbed
As I peered into the darkness around me
I began fighting to reclaim the surface, but
I was so far from the light all I could see was twilight
I was in free fall, sinking deeper and deeper
Into the abyss of hopelessness and depression
I felt a coldness and saw a darkness I never thought possible
I hit an equilibrium point where I felt I was no longer sinking
But my thoughts began to remind me of why I was here
I was so tired of fighting
I was so tired of trying to prove myself as a man
I was so tired of searching for love and companionship
I was so tired of being unhappy and hurt
I was so tired of being disappointed and
Being someone else's disappointment
I was so tired of living the street life
I was so tired masking with drugs
I was so tired of feeling like a mouse trapped in a maze
That had no way out
I was so tired of waking up to this endless nightmare
My will was faint like my heartbeat
Similar to the day I was born
Deep in depression
I was ready to surrender to the peace and
Quiet I've eluded so many times in my waking hours
At the perfect moment
I threw myself in front of a Mack Truck traveling at high speed

Wearing all black at night in torrential rain
I don't know how the driver saw me
When I could hardly see myself
The rain pelted my face like small stones falling from the sky
I don't know how the driver could have stopped on a dime
He was carrying a full load and the truck didn't skid or jackknife
The driver jumped out of his rig and
Ran toward me in the pouring rain
He kept a little distance between us, but yelled
What the hell is wrong with you?
Are you crazy?
We both could have been killed!
He ran back to his rig soaking wet and started to drive off
At that moment I knew it was **divine intervention**
I knew it wasn't my time to go
I knew I was loved and protected by the **most high**
I knew there was more to be done with my life
I knew I had a purpose in life to fulfill
Just as my light was about be extinguished
I was given a second chance to live and view life with new eyes

I was blessed to have multiple chances at living and getting my life right. Don't waste your first attempt! Many are not given a second chance!

CHAPTER 3

BRILLANCE: The Awakening

"As I began to wake up and see the errors in my ways

I realized what I was doing to myself and those around me

I began to shed my hurtful and destructive behaviors

Like leaves, broken tree limbs and twigs

Falling to the ground daily"

Christopher Allen

Awakening

As I began to wake up and see the errors in my ways
I saw what I was doing to myself and those around me
I began to shed my hurtful and destructive behaviors
Like leaves, broken tree limbs and twigs
Falling to the ground daily

Compartmentalized

Since man was able to pass lineages and
History through cultural stories
Carve, chisel, and draw symbols and
Visuals onto rocks, clay, and cave walls
Men were groomed from the time we were born
To be hunters, the head of household, leaders,
The breadwinners, disciplinarians
The protectors, warriors, and scholars
From day one
It has been engraved in our young men
Not to show any fear, weakness, mercy and never cry
Men were not taught to deal with the emotional and
Feminine aspects of his being, but there they are
This is an epidemic problem that needs to be
Revisited, changed, and retaught
We need to teach our young men that
It is unnatural to become a walking time bomb
Exploding unsuspectedly in the lives of our loved ones
And strangers
Emotions should not be compartmentalized or suppressed
Stored, hidden, or locked away
Like some dark secret
Emotions are a part of our lives
It is not a secret
It is in our nature
It is okay to cry
It is okay to be vulnerable
It is okay to feel sad
It is okay to love and be loved
It is okay to be compassionate
It is okay to be happy
It is okay to smile
It is okay to accept help from others
These emotions are not weaknesses
It is a part of us, like our hair, fingers, eyes, and toes
It is okay to feel and express our emotions
In a constructive and positive way
Not just through hate, anger, bitterness, and frustration

I don't have all the answers, but we have to address the issue of how we raise our young me in today's society!

I Made a Mistake

A mistake is misspelling a word wrong
A mistake is putting together a TV stand and it leans to one side
A mistake is dropping a cup of coffee on the floor by accident
A mistake is pronouncing someone's name wrong
The reason is because your thoughts and
Actions were not intended in a negative way
You cannot say that cheating on a test was a mistake
You cannot say that stealing from someone or a store
Is a mistake
You cannot say that lying is a mistake
You cannot say that hollering at someone is a mistake
You cannot say that putting your hands on someone is a mistake
You cannot say that killing someone is a mistake
You cannot say that blaming something on someone else
Knowing that it was all your fault is not a mistake
Why?
Because you made a conscious choice and decision
To commit an act with negative intent

Be careful of your intent and what you claim to be a mistake because the mistake that you make won't be an excuse to the public eye, jury, judge or family!

I'm Sorry

Dean,

      My anger, frustration, and fight weren't toward you growing up. It was towards my biological father. I thank you for your continued love, support, and patience. Thank you for being there for me in his absence. You were a good, honest, reliable, and hardworking man. You didn't deserve the brunt of my pain, rebellion, and negative behaviors. Over the years I'm glad we had a chance to bond, talk, respect, and understand one another like a father and son should. I told you then and I proclaim it to the world now that I love you and I'm sorry!

Your son,

Christopher Allen

Who Do You Have to Blame?

Young men and women
It was a fault of my biological father
For not being a major part of my life
At times I was a complete mess without him, but
I cannot and will not blame him for the decisions I made in my life
He wasn't there when we all made good choices
We wouldn't give him credit for that
Nor was he there when we made bad choices
Why should we give him credit for that?
He didn't hold a gun to our heads forcing us to do what we did
I did it
You did it
We did it
If you were to look back in the past
And see all of your mistakes
Who do you have to blame?

You are responsible for choices, behavior and actions in every aspect of your life. No one else is responsible, you are!

The Loss of Choice and Freedom

When you do something wrong to someone or offend another
You lose the choice and freedom of what happens to you next
You don't get to decide on how they should react, respond
Or treat you regardless of what we think, how we feel
Or the rights we think we have under the constitution
Don't sacrifice your choice and freedom
By losing your cool in the moment
Because when it's all said and done
You will realize it was all over nothing and
It all could have been avoided
Often times it's too late to go back and
Change what we should have said or
Change what we should have done in that moment
So please don't let anger, pride, or peer pressure
Take you down a path where your words and actions
Cause you to lose your choice of peace, life, and freedom

Badge of Honor

There's no badge of honor in having children that
You can't take care of just for a few moments of pleasure
Or just to say that you had sex with someone
Regardless of your age
Sex doesn't make you into a man or a woman
It's a gender classification
Nor does it provide you the know how to be a mother or father
There's no badge of honor for not getting an education or
Learning how to read and write
You are fully capable of learning and
Achieving anything you put your mind to do
There is no badge of honor for being rude or disrespectful
It won't cost you a dime to treat people nicely or smile
There is no badge of honor in breaking your curfew
There is nothing good happening in the streets after 9 p.m.
There is no badge of honor in disregarding the rules of your home
You can do whatever you want to
When you become grown and get your own
There is no badge of honor
In expecting someone to take care of you past the age of 18
You are considered an adult
Prepare to be treated as you wished underneath your breath
Many nights in your parent or parents' home
There is no badge of honor in selling or using drugs
It diminishes the chances of you achieving
Your goals and being successful in life
There is no badge of honor in taking a human life
Remember, the life you took was someone's child,
Brother, sister, father, mother, cousin, uncle, aunt, or grandparent
There's no badge of honor in
Trading your life for a jail or prison suit
You'll be going before your Honor
With your code and honor
Saying your Honor
Getting a high count in years
Like the peoples' personal use of marijuana
Over having a masked persona

To be cool, liked, or just to fit in
All for a badge of honor that doesn't exist

My Girl's Friends Confession

Girl, I wish I had a man that looked at me the way he looks at you
I wish I had a man that worked steadily and
Did right by me and my children
Meaning, accepting, and treating them like they were his own
I wish I had a man that would take me out on dates and
Take me to his work functions
Whether I'm politically suitable for the occasion or not
I wish I had a man that was honest and told me the truth
As opposed to playing games and telling lies
I wish I had a man that supported my dreams and aspirations
I wish I had a man that wanted to get to know me
Instead of lusting after my silhouette in jeans, flats, or heels
I wish I had a man that accepts me for who I am
Flaws and all, right here and now
I wish I had a man that talks to me respectfully, listens and
Tries to understand me
Without always jumping to conclusions or casting judgment
I wish I had a man that really appreciated all I have to offer
I wish I had a man that was solely committed to me and no one else
Girl, you have it all and don't even know it
It is a damn shame you don't appreciate what you have
You act like you don't want him, but that's okay
I'll gladly take him any day
Over the knuckleheads and bullshit out here in these streets

Just for the Moment

Is it a fact that
People are who they are and do not change
But change temporarily to undo or ease an
Uncomfortable outcome or situation?
Just for the moment
They are the greatest actors without winning an Oscar
They are so sincere
Letting the tears flow
Just pretending
Even better liars
Masters of the game
Their manipulations on fleek
They are always the victim
Lovers of many
But they love no one not even themselves

Acceptance and Forgiveness

When you started all of this
I wasn't rude or disrespectful to you
Despite the way I truly felt and
What I could have done to you
Be thankful for my decency and restraint
Because I've come too far to allow someone's
Behavior to change the course of my life
No one is worthy of that, but
My acceptance of your apology and my forgiveness
Won't be based on your time or terms
Because the work I got for you is free like interns
My boys wanted to burn you like pure grade perm
For every wrong there's consequences and
A lesson to be learned
And every time I think about it
I get flustered
But I know Karma can be a real bad mother
So, I forgive you and when I see you
I may speak to you, but I definitely won't be dealing with you

Because of people like you
My circle has become small
Down to a pinheads view
I don't have to touch you
Just know it will come back to you

It is very important to forgive and be forgiven!

The Urban Male Disorder

Whenever I was dating a woman that had a child or
Children by another man and
He wasn't in a relationship with the woman or
Involved with his children
Once he saw how I interacted with them and
The woman he still had feelings for
He saw potential in us to be what he always wanted for himself

His jealously and desire to reclaim what he failed to sustain
By not giving her his last name
He pretended to step up and be a father to his children
He pretended to be a changed man
He tried to befriend us both and regain her trust
He had hoped to sweep her off her feet and win her back
But as a man, I knew the plan and the games began
When he couldn't find a way to win her back
He began to show his true scent and colors, piss yellow
It's a shame he became an eraser smudge
In the minds and lives of his children and ex-love
The good father and friendship routine
Got played out like butterfly collars and politicians
If he had remained a parent and
Left his fantasies and regrets out of the picture
He could have repaired the relationships he had broken
Some time ago
But instead, he lost sight of what was really important
Trying to size me up
As if he really had a chance of beating me or getting her back
Somehow, I became the reasons and excuses as to why
He wasn't a presence in his children's lives!

 # The Urban Male Disorder # In Denial # Deadbeats # Sperm Donors # Selfish # Jealous # Haters # Move on # Be a father # Get your life together

The moral of the poem is just because you are not in relationship or digging out your child or children's mother isn't an excuse to disregard your responsibilities as a father!

Put Down the Gun

Your lack of direction, character, ignorance, and laziness
Pointing the finger at others, bad attitude
Poor self-esteem, selfishness, and sense of entitlement
Are the excuses and tools that you keep using
To build your bad life
You are the bullets in the clip
That riddle and render your God given temple and talent useless
Put down the gun

Although obstacles exist, you are the only one standing in front of it. Go over, through or around your obstacles! Become solution based instead of victim or excuse based!

In My Opinion

In my opinion
No man, woman or child are born a racist
We are taught to be a racist
We learn the excuses, the language, and the behaviors
To be accepted in our families, cultures, and communities
Who truly acts and thinks like this from birth?

In my opinion
When you become of age and
You know right from wrong in your heart
You have a choice to change for the better good
Educate others to end this senseless hate, violence, and nonsense
Plant seeds of unity and life in our communities and beyond
One individual at time

Desensitized

Today I am not completely happy with the many termed
Afro-Americans
And melanins who haven't studied, dismissed or forgotten their
history and heritage
A time of slavery, atrocity, peril, and struggle
Over four hundred plus years of division, pain, and tears
And yes, it is still here
Today, the agendas are being carried out in a different way
It is the poisoning of our food and water
The illusions of freedom of choice
Attacking us through media, and music
Supposed education and our economic systems
Many of us are not proud of our skin color or heritage
Our youth are clueless, brainwashed, distracted, and desensitized
To our past and current struggles
Widely accepting the partially and
Falsely written histories of our people and culture
Do your research and discover the truth
Because God knows that one conversation or book won't do it
I'm not promoting violence or
Stating we should hate our perpetrators
But together we must stand and
Hold the government and its subsidiaries accountable
For equal rights, the reporting of true history and
The proper treatment of our people

Separated

We are separated at birth
Separated by deceit
Separated by relationships
Separated by race
Separated by gender
Separated by color
Separated by our looks
Separated by culture
Separated by language
Separated by beliefs
Separated by education
Separated by money
Separated by material things
Separated by credit
Separated by land
Separated by countries
Separated by water
Separated by neighborhoods
Separated by religion
Separated by class
Separated from nature
Separated by media
Separated by TV
Separated by music
Separated by propaganda
Separated by talent
Separated by fashion
Separated by clothes
Separated by hate
Separated by pain
Separated by greed
Separated by mistrust
Separated by fear
Separated by jealousy
Separated by pride
Separated by ego
Separated by crime
Separated by prisons

Separated from our families
Separated by identity
Separated by race
Separated by government
Separated by war
Separated by sickness
Separated by death
And the only time we unite
Is if we need something from one another
Or someone you care about, or love passes away
We have been conditioned to be separated and
Divided against one another
Together we stand and divided we fall
When will we learn to unify and
Overcome division in a separatist society?

Change

Its amazes me that people always notice
How you change towards them
But they never want to acknowledge or talk
About what they have done to you to cause the change

The Truth

I would rather know the truth than to hear a lie,
But the reality of it for most people
Is that knowing the truth and living with it
Can be more painful and difficult
Then living with a lie

Often, I Find Myself

Often, I find myself putting the world on mute
I use this time to reflect and listen to my inner self
I find myself not taking anything personal anymore
I can't expect everyone to react, behave or respond
The way that I feel, think, and conduct myself
I find myself reinforcing my beliefs through actions
And through action my character comes to light
And is recognized by true eyes
I find myself taking long showers because
It seems to drain and wash away the grit
I've accumulated throughout the day
Mentally, emotionally, and physically
I find myself alone at times
Because there's not many people on my level of existence
I find myself being hated for being responsible as a man and
Being conscious of others' thoughts and feelings
I find myself being ridiculed
For not associating myself with trivial people
And superficial things
I find myself having to watch what I say to those
Whose realities are based on fallacies and not the truth
Often, I find myself

Sometimes

Sometimes when the enemy attempt to get me out of character
Sometimes when I become angry
Sometimes when I'm tempted
I turn the other way shake my head and just smile

The same actions and reactions
I would have done in the past
Cross my mind like sprinters at the finish line
But for the sake of having a peace of mind
For the sake of not suppressing secrets and lies
For the sake of not having to look over my shoulders
For the sake of not having to cover my tracks
For the sake of not carrying the burden of guilt
For the sake of not being caught up in some mess
I can walk away with my head up high and just smile

Complacent Breeze

There have been periods in my life
Where I was very passionate and
I walked amongst the clouds in high pursuit of
My goals, dreams, and aspirations
There were also times when I lost control of my flight
And I descended uncontrollably to a complacent breeze
A motivational freeze, becoming stagnant
I had become that Dandelion Seedling
Being taken up into the air and blown into any direction
I was floating and flowing to a complacent breeze
Moving and swirling here and there
With no purpose, direction, or destination to go
Dangling in the gallows of doubt and self-pity
For not achieving what I thought I should have
At this point in my life
As the clouds and rain of yesteryear reappear
I am replenished with new dreams, goals, and aspirations
All sprouting exuberantly
I am transforming my life from dreamer to achiever
Using this complacent breeze as a means
To soar to new heights and
Reach achievements beyond my wildest dreams

Don't ever stop dreaming and making realistic plans to create and obtain those dreams!

Idle Time

Sitting idle
I become dizzy with emotion
My mistakes, failures, and issues
Began to spin in my mind like a time elapsed video
And the lens was pointed up at the night sky
Every star in the sky is a spec on my conscious
Staining my mind and self-esteem like iodine
Wherever I turn, there is nowhere to run or hide
You cannot escape from yourself
I am faced with an unseen judge and jury that hand out and
Whisper sentences longer than the sentences I write daily
Voices tell me that I am unworthy
And I'm far from being saved like Christians
And paragraphs in word documents
The voices never stop like fanatics and rituals
Attacking and reminding me of everything I've done is habitual
So, if I allow myself to act out and feel this way about myself
Will the world treat me the same?
So, I walk around with Photoshop
Crop, edit, and improve myself
Giving the world the best that I've got
Meaning, if you don't take responsibility, and
Heal the root of your pain
It will find a way to deal with you in idle time

Your Legacy

In the midst of our life's storms, it is easy to lose sight of our dreams and purpose as we pick up the pieces to rebuild our foundation. During this rebuilding phase, if I were asked the following questions sooner, I believe that the focus and direction of my life may have significantly changed a long time ago.

If you were to leave this Earth today, what would people say about you? What is your legacy? What is your plan to build your legacy? Who would you leave it to and why?

You are never too young or too old to understand what your life's purpose is and manifest that purpose into your legacy! Being empowered and influencing others to do the same are the seeds we need growing everywhere, right now!

In Reflection

Reflection is a serious thought or consideration. Many sources say that it is a change in direction of light, sound, waves, or energy back to the source it came from. In reflection, many individuals don't realize that what you harbor internally and put out verbally, mentally, and emotionally will come back to you. In many aspects, my life reflected my belief systems and the energy I put out.

In reflection of my life experiences, I truly had to accept that life is not perfect, or fair. It is about how you respond to the tests that come your way and being thankful for your victories, both large and small. Realizing that, how are you handling you're challenges? How are you processing it? What are you projecting from it, positivity, and growth, or negativity? It took some time, but I applied what I learned below to help me maintain peace of mind and remain accountable for my thoughts and actions.

- Living happily forever after is not realistic
- People's perceptions about you and your life experiences don't define you
- Don't allow negative emotions, thoughts or experiences consume you
- Feel and go through your emotions, but don't stay in them
- Think before reacting
- Trust your instincts and intuition
- Never lose yourself in a relationship
- Love yourself enough to say *NO* and *Goodbye*
- Don't be afraid to be alone
- When someone shows you who they are believe it
- Get away from people that don't mean you well
- Continuously re-evaluate your personal, intimate, and business relationships
- Maintain your peace, character, and professionalism

- Never do anything that you are ashamed of or wouldn't want someone else to find out
- Learn and grow from your mistakes
- Stop expecting things you can't give or won't do for another
- Judge and ye shall be judged
- Communicate, people can't read your mind
- Never lose sight of your dreams, achieve them
- Change the negative patterns and narratives in your life
- Respect other thoughts and opinions
- Meet each individual where they are not where you think they should be
- Create boundaries to control yourself not others
- Transparency is the key to healing

You can do the same, but first, apply these to your life and see the positive changes that will take place on your journey.

In reflection, I am very humble and grateful to be here today to share my story. Please leave a short review or comment on my website, social media platforms or by email. I will read all your reviews and comments personally. Your responses and reviews are important to me. Your feedback will make a huge difference in the development of future works.

About the Author

Christopher Allen is public notary, author, publisher, producer, mentor, actor, model, and speaker, dedicating many of his works and time to inspire personal growth, community, healthy relationships, fatherhood, mindfulness, self-worth, and inner healing.

Born in Charleston, West Virginia, Christopher was raised on the Eastern Shores of Maryland and Delaware. Later, he took up residence in Philadelphia to further his career as an actor, model, writer, songwriter, and poet before moving to Richmond, Virginia in 2007. In 2016, he obtained a paralegal degree specializing in Litigation E-Discovery. Prior to graduating, he also wrote three books; A Guide to Open Wounds, and two editions titled, Open Wounds. One version is dedicated to adult men and the other is dedicated to male youth, ages 8 to 18. He is currently working on two additional books called Bottlely Harm and a children's series focusing on reducing anxiety and childhood trauma. His works are published by Ascension Publishing, LLC. In addition, he is writing in tandem with creative minds to produce new works for several web series, plays, and movies. He is currently the Vice President of Entrepreneurs and Business Owners, Editorial Manager for the Healing Connector, a member of Black Male Emergent Readers, and Producer of the Issues of Men platform. He uses his voice and gifts to bring about positive changes in the lives of others. He has spoken at schools, colleges, churches, venues, radio shows and social media platforms to share his message and story.

Contact Information

Web: www.authorchrisallen.com/home
Twitter: @CAllenAuthor
IG: authorchristopherallen
Email: authorchristopherallen@gmail.com

Ascension Publishing, LLC
For services
Email: ascensionpublishingllc@gmail.com
Tel: 804-212-5347